Opening up
Exodus

IAIN D CAMPBELL

Opening up
Exodus

IAIN D CAMPBELL

'This is a fine introduction to the study of the Book of Exodus. It fits particularly well with those who have little knowledge of the exodus account and story. It will be particularly helpful in Bible study groups and in youth groups. The study questions at the end of each chapter will help to facilitate discussion of the issues raised in Exodus. I heartily recommend it as a starting place for the study of this important book of the Old Testament.'

John D Currid
Reformed Theological Seminary, Jackson, Mississippi

'This study is a most helpful and interesting introduction to the book of Exodus. In style it meets Calvin's standard of lucid brevity. In focus it shows the structure and meaning of the book as a whole. In theology it is reliable and orthodox. It also contains the rarest of features: excellent discussion questions. I recommend it highly.'

W Robert Godfrey
Professor of Church History and President of Westminster Seminary California

© Day One Publications 2006

First printed 2006

Scripture quotations, unless otherwise indicated, are from The Holy Bible, English Standard Version, copyright © 2001 by Crossway Bibles, a division of Good News Publishers. Used by permission. All rights reserved."

ISBN 1 84625 029 -3

British Library Cataloguing in Publication Data available

Published by Day One Publications
Ryelands Road, Leominster, HR6 8NZ
Telephone 01568 613 740   FAX 01568 611 473

email—sales@dayone.co.uk
web site—www.dayone.co.uk
North American—e-mail-sales@dayonebookstore.com
North American web site—www.dayonebookstore.com

All rights reserved

No part of this publication may be reproduced, or stored in a retrieval system, or transmitted, in any form or by any means, mechanical, electronic, photocopying, recording or otherwise, without the prior permission of Day One Publications.

Designed by Steve Devane and printed by Gutenberg Press, Malta

For my friends and colleagues

O. Palmer Robertson and Kenneth J. Mackenzie

and all involved with them

in the development of African Bible College, Uganda

Exodus 36:1-2

List of Bible abbreviations

THE OLD TESTAMENT		1 Chr.	1 Chronicles	Dan.	Daniel
		2 Chr.	2 Chronicles	Hosea	Hosea
Gen.	Genesis	Ezra	Ezra	Joel	Joel
Exod.	Exodus	Neh.	Nehemiah	Amos	Amos
Lev.	Leviticus	Esth.	Esther	Obad.	Obadiah
Num.	Numbers	Job	Job	Jonah	Jonah
Deut.	Deuteronomy	Ps.	Psalms	Micah	Micah
Josh.	Joshua	Prov.	Proverbs	Nahum	Nahum
Judg.	Judges	Eccles.	Ecclesiastes	Hab.	Habakkuk
Ruth	Ruth	S.of.S.	Song of Solomon	Zeph.	Zephaniah
1 Sam.	1 Samuel	Isa.	Isaiah	Hag.	Haggai
2 Sam.	2 Samuel	Jer.	Jeremiah	Zech.	Zechariah
1 Kings	1 Kings	Lam.	Lamentations	Mal.	Malachi
2 Kings	2 Kings	Ezek.	Ezekiel		

THE NEW TESTAMENT		Gal.	Galatians	Heb.	Hebrews
		Eph.	Ephesians	James	James
Matt.	Matthew	Phil.	Philippians	1 Peter	1 Peter
Mark	Mark	Col.	Colossians	2 Peter	2 Peter
Luke	Luke	1 Thes.	1 Thessalonians	1 John	1 John
John	John	2 Thes.	2 Thessalonians	2 John	2 John
Acts	Acts	1 Tim.	1 Timothy	3 John	3 John
Rom.	Romans	2 Tim.	2 Timothy	Jude	Jude
1 Cor.	1 Corinthians	Titus	Titus	Rev.	Revelation
2 Cor.	2 Corinthians	Philem.	Philemon		

Overview

The Book of Exodus tells an important story. The word 'exodus' literally means 'a way out'; and that is precisely what the second book of the Bible describes—the God who provided 'a way out' for his people, who were slaves in Egypt. Central to that story is the character of Moses, whom God prepares and then calls to challenge Pharaoh, to lead God's people out of slavery, and to be their leader in the first stage of their journey towards the promised land. Central, too, is the defining meeting with God at Mount Sinai, where God spoke to his people, giving them laws and constituting them a theocracy—a nation which was to be holy, set apart for God's worship and service.

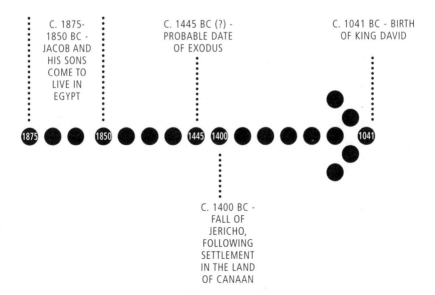

C. 1875-1850 BC - JACOB AND HIS SONS COME TO LIVE IN EGYPT

C. 1445 BC (?) - PROBABLE DATE OF EXODUS

C. 1041 BC - BIRTH OF KING DAVID

C. 1400 BC - FALL OF JERICHO, FOLLOWING SETTLEMENT IN THE LAND OF CANAAN

1875 1850 1445 1400 1041

OPENING UP EXODUS

Introduction

The Book of Exodus is the second part of a five-part work, which is made up of the Books of Genesis, Exodus, Leviticus, Numbers and Deuteronomy. When Jesus said that 'everything written about me in the Law of Moses and the Prophets and the Psalms must be fulfilled' (Luke 24:44), he was using the Jewish division of the Scriptures into three parts: Law, Prophets and Writings. 'The Law of Moses' is the first major section of the Old Testament.

Exodus, therefore, must be studied both in the light of what Genesis has already said, and what the rest of the 'Law of Moses' says. It begins with a reference to the past (1:1-8) and ends with a reference to the future (40:38). In between, it tells a remarkable story about God breaking into the experience of his people, to deliver them from slavery and set them apart as his own.

God reveals himself by words and actions

The Book of Exodus is about God and what he does for his people. As with the rest of the Bible, Exodus is part of God's revelation of himself to us. Unless God reveals himself to us, we can never know what he is like. And it is Jesus himself who tells us that eternal life means knowing God (John 17:3).

In Exodus, God reveals himself in two ways: by what he SAYS and by what he DOES. We hear God speaking: he speaks to Moses, but he also speaks *through* Moses to his people. Moses, therefore, is cast in the role of a PROPHET. God's words are communicated to his people, and as he speaks, God makes himself known.

But Exodus is also about the God who reveals himself in his *actions*. He breaks into the history, in order to lead his people out of slavery. His plagues over Egypt are designed to show that he alone is God (Exod. 7:5). As He displays his power, he shows himself to be God.

What we know about God, therefore, we know because he has spoken and because he has acted in human history. That is particularly true of Jesus, who is the Word (John 1:1—the *speech* of God), but who is also the one who saves. In Jesus, as in Exodus, God reveals himself by speaking and by action.

The role of Moses

As well as being the author of Exodus, Moses is central to the story of Exodus. We read about his birth, his call and his subsequent role as the Mediator of God's covenant and the Saviour of God's people. Although the Book of Exodus is not about Moses, it is nonetheless a book in which he has a substantial role to play.

Meredith Kline has suggested that the way Moses is portrayed in Exodus parallels the way Jesus is portrayed in the Gospels. In fact, he suggests that the Gospel writers may well have borrowed from the Old Testament as they wrote of the birth, life and death of the Son of God.

Consider the following parallels. In the case of Moses and Jesus, we know:

About their birth and miraculous preservation;

Very little about them between the time of their birth and their public ministry;

About their public call and commission;

About their work in redemption and salvation.

What Moses was in the Old Testament, Jesus is in the New. Hebrews chapter 3 explicitly compares and contrasts them: both of them serve the Lord faithfully, Moses as God's servant and Jesus as God's son (Heb. 3:5-6). Yet the reality is that Moses was a kind of foreshadowing of the Christ who was to come. Therefore, we are to 'consider Jesus, who was faithful to him that appointed him, just as Moses also was faithful in all God's house' (Heb. 3:2).

The relation between Moses and Christ is further brought out in the Book of Revelation, where we are told that the saints in heaven

sing the song of Moses, the servant of God, and the song of the Lamb, saying,

'Great and amazing are your deeds, O Lord God Almighty!

Just and true are your ways, O King of the nations!

Who will not fear, O Lord, and glorify your name?

For you alone are holy.

All nations will come and worship you, for your righteous acts have been revealed' (Rev. 15:3-4).

Therefore, as we go through the Book of Exodus, we will see the different ways in which Christ's work is brought before us. Just as he taught others to see the things that the Law of Moses said about him, so we will try to see them too.

The gospel in Exodus

This brings us to another issue: the question of *types* and *typology*. The word 'type' here has nothing to do with mechanical writing or with the quality of something. Its meaning is quite different.

When we study the Book of Exodus and its history, we pay attention to the events that unfolded at the time. We look at the context in which the history took place: events that occurred in Egypt and elsewhere, the life of Moses, and so on. But we also study that history in the wider context of the Bible, taking the Bible as a unit, and taking its storyline as telling one simple story of salvation. The Bible tells of how God stepped in from the moment man sinned, to deliver man from the results of his rebellious actions against God. In successive generations, and in different ways, God worked in the history of the world, preparing the world for the coming of Jesus Christ, whose death and resurrection would finally deal with the problem of man's sin.

> In successive generations, and in different ways, God worked in the history of the world, preparing the world for the coming of Jesus Christ, whose death and resurrection would finally deal with the problem of man's sin.

One consequence of this is that some of the things God

gave to and did for his people, of which we have a record in the Book of Exodus, were not simply powerful elements of the revelation of his grace at the time, but were intended to point forward to, and illustrate the redeeming work of Christ. Woven into the history of the Old Testament are people, places, names, rituals and actions which have a deep meaning in themselves, and an even deeper significance in the light of the Bible's unifying storyline and theme. These people, places and rituals are not simply important in themselves; they are important as *types*, or images which anticipate something greater in the future.

Geerhardus Vos, who taught theology in America in the nineteenth century, always insisted that in order to find out whether something is a *type* of the future, you have first to ask what it *symbolized* at the time. One of his illustrations was that 'the gateway to the house of typology is at the farther end of the house of symbolism'.[1] In other words, the Bible reader has to put himself or herself in the shoes of those whom the history describes and ask, 'What would this have symbolized?' Then, having worked through the symbolism, we can find the typology.

Take, for example, the fact of the redemption from Egypt. What did these great events symbolize? That God determined to save his people out of their slavery by the death of a substitutionary lamb. That was what the people knew. That was the provision made for them. But we, with the greater light of the complete Bible, can say that that is God's way of saving us, too—through the death of a substitute. And when the Bible calls Christ the Lamb of God (John 1:29, 36; Rev. 5:6) and our passover (1 Cor. 5:7), we realize that the events of Exodus anticipated the future, and the coming of Jesus Christ. They were *types* of his redeeming work; with the perfect atonement of his providing, these types were fulfilled, and were no longer necessary.

Similarly, we can look at the role of Moses in Exodus and say: here is a *type*, a prefigurement of the great Saviour and Commander of God's people, the Lord Jesus Christ. Moses, to be sure, had his faults, unlike Jesus, and yet we can find points of comparison between them. As a prophet, Moses is a type of Jesus, the greatest, and last, of all God's prophets. As a deliverer, Moses is a type of the delivering, liberating work of Jesus. He symbolized God's personal commitment to save his people; and in that symbolism he represents the One who is the only Person who can truly set sinners free.

Or take the Tabernacle as another example. The Tabernacle represented the presence of God with his people. It was a symbol of the God who could dwell among his own people, even though the glory of his holiness threatened to destroy them at Sinai. That was the surface meaning of the Tabernacle; yet it represented a principle that has now been fulfilled in Jesus, who is 'Immanuel ... God with us' (Matt. 1:23). Therefore we can say that the Tabernacle was a *type* of Christ, full of wonderful redemptive significance and meaning.

There is a danger in all of this, of course. Typology does not mean that we must find hidden meanings where there are none. The Bible is not a code to be cracked. But it is a wonderfully full, coherent and unified book, in which the Old Testament and the New cast a remarkable light on each other. As we try to open up Exodus in the following chapters, we need to study Exodus in its own light, and also in the light of what Christ has done for us. In O.P. Robertson's words, 'the covenant of law consummates in Jesus Christ'.[2]

Problems over dating

There is one other issue that deserves comment. That is the vexed problem over when the events of Exodus took place.[3]

Part of the problem focuses on 1 Kings 6:1, which dates Solomon's building of the Temple in this way:

> In the four hundred and eightieth year after the people of Israel came out of the land of Egypt, in the fourth year of Solomon's reign over Israel, in the month of Ziv, which is the second month, he began to build the house of the LORD.

If this chronology is correct, then that would date the exodus around 1445 BC, since we know that Solomon began to reign in 971 BC. However, scholars tend to argue that the exodus should be dated later, around 1290 BC. It is possible that the information in 1 Kings 6:1 is approximate, reckoning 12 generations of 40 years each. By reducing the number of years reckoned to make up a generation, one can then arrive at a later date for the exodus. However, in an extended article in his *Encyclopedia of Bible Difficulties*, Gleason Archer argued that after an 'extensive survey of the biblical, historical and archaeological evidence, we are forced to conclude that only the 1445 [BC] date can be sustained'.[4]

The difficulties in reconstructing the history do not, however, argue against the truthfulness of the biblical account. They merely alert us to the fact that much ancient history cannot be accurately chronicled by us until a great deal more material comes to light. But, whatever the problems caused by dating, all the biblical writers who allude to it assume the historical trustworthiness of the Exodus account.

Structure

The Book of Exodus is going to take us on a journey out of Egypt and into the desert. It is going to tell us about a God who never goes back on his covenant promise and commitment, about a God who acts as King to deliver his people from the power of another king and the bondage of another kingdom. We will first of all be introduced to the King's people, covenanted to God but slaves to Pharaoh. We will meet one special person, Moses, chosen by God from among his covenant people to be their leader, guardian and saviour. We will see how God fulfilled his covenant promise by equipping Moses with power and commissioning him to challenge Pharaoh and his gods.

We will then follow the King as he leads his people out of Egypt, providing all that they need to escape his judgement on the land, to face the obstacles in their path, and to survive in the harsh environment of the desert. And we will camp with Israel at Mount Sinai, where the people of God will have a meeting with their King, where they will hear his voice and receive his laws. We will observe as the King renews his covenant pledge and confirms his covenant promise to his people.

And then we will see how the King purposes to be present with his people, dwelling alongside them in a tent, where his name and his glory will reside. We will see how he calls his covenant people to walk in his way, and to keep his company.

We will discover how easily they drift out of his way into false worship and idolatry. And we will marvel at the King's gracious love to his own people as he leads them on.

As we do so, we will learn the basic vocabulary of the gospel. It's an interesting and important fact that almost all the words that are important in the New Testament in explaining the gospel to us are before us in the Book of Exodus. So as we follow the people of God on their 'journey of a lifetime', we will pause every so often to learn the 'ABC', the building blocks of the good news, the vocabulary in which the message of God's salvation is communicated to us.

Let's begin by meeting the King's people.

FOR FURTHER STUDY

1. Psalms 78, 80, 81, 105, 106, 114, 135 and 136 all refer to the exodus from Egypt. What do these psalms tell us about the God of the Book of Exodus?

2. In Acts 7, Stephen refers to the events of the Book of Exodus as part of his defence as a Christian. What is our relationship in Christ to the events of this book?

TO THINK ABOUT AND DISCUSS

1. 'A covenant commits people to one another'.[5] How often does the idea of a covenant appear in Exodus? How does the theme of the covenant in Exodus reveal to us the extent of God's commitment to his people, and of them to him?

2. Is it possible to preach the gospel on the basis of the events in the Book of Exodus? What does this book teach us about the elements of God's salvation?

3. What do you think the Christian attitude to the law of God ought to be in this age of the Holy Spirit?

PART 1

Meeting the King's People

1 Covenant People

(1:1-22)

Exodus 1 acts as a bridge between the events of Genesis and the story of God's redemption in history. It is a reminder that the story is continuing: the promises of salvation from Genesis are now worked out in the events which follow.

The first chapter of Exodus is our introduction to the storyline of this great book. It sets the context for us, explaining to us the situation in which God's people found themselves, and why they needed rescuing. Into the hopelessness of their situation, God was going to bring his power and grace, to provide them with a way out. So read on, to recap on some of the events that went before, and to see what the need is now.

Introduction (1:1-7)

These opening verses of Exodus summarize events that took place about seventy years before, when Jacob came to Egypt

(Gen. 46). By providing this link with the past, they serve to remind us that Exodus is going to continue the story begun in Genesis.

Interestingly, in the first verse, the two names of the father of the tribes are given. First, he is called *Israel*, and then *Jacob*. Israel was the name God gave Jacob in Genesis 35:10, and it was the name which was to be identified particularly with the people and the land of God's covenant blessing.

Joseph, 1:5 tells us, was already in Egypt when his father and brothers joined him to live there. The remarkable story of Joseph's rise from obscurity to royalty is told in Genesis 37-50. Although it began with the hatred of his brothers against him, plotting to kill him and eventually selling him off as a slave, it ended with the realization that God had higher plans and purposes. Joseph could say to his brothers, 'God sent me before you to preserve for you a remnant on earth, and to keep alive for you many survivors. So it was not you who sent me here, but God' (Gen. 45:7-8).

Joseph's position in Egypt was such that he was able to provide for his family when a famine struck the land. God's hand was in all these events, and his blessing was evident in the way in which the descendants of Jacob grew in number, and filled the land of Egypt (1:7).

Slaves under Pharaoh (1:8-14)

The situation for the children of Israel drastically altered with the appearance of a Pharaoh who was not interested in Joseph or what he had done for his people. He was driven by political and practical motives to ensure that the Israelites would not grow in number (1:9), and thus overcome the

Egyptians. His first strategy was to make them serve Egypt by building-programmes which were designed to compel their loyalty.

The effect was the opposite: 'the more they were oppressed, the more they multiplied' (1:12). Pharaoh added to their burden, making them slaves and setting cruel taskmasters over them.

Faithful to God (1:15-22)

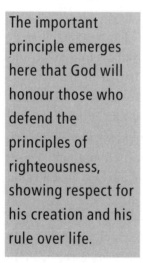

The important principle emerges here that God will honour those who defend the principles of righteousness, showing respect for his creation and his rule over life.

In spite of the dangers involved, there were some who proved themselves faithful to God. Pharaoh decreed that the Israelite boys should be killed at birth. This infanticide was too horrible to contemplate, so two midwives, Shiphrah and Puah, refused to comply. Even before Pharaoh, they showed their shrewdness and their respect for human life, claiming that the Israelite women gave birth quickly, before the midwives could come to help them.

The important principle emerges here that God will honour those who defend the principles of righteousness, showing respect for his creation and his rule over life. The midwives are more anxious to please God than to please Pharaoh, and God rewards them.

Pharaoh's plan then turns nasty, as he commands that the sons of the Israelites be drowned in the River Nile (1:22).

FOR FURTHER STUDY

1. Why does God ask his people to remember that they were slaves in Egypt in Deuteronomy 5:15? What about in Deuteronomy 24:18?

2. Both Jesus (in John 8:34) and Paul (in Rom. 6:16) compare the condition of those who commit sin to a condition of slavery. Do you think the situation of the children of Israel in Egypt sheds light for us on what that condition involves?

3. What parallels can you find between the treatment which Pharaoh gave to the Israelite children in Exodus 1, and the way King Herod treated the Israelite children of a future generation (Matt. 2:16-18)?

TO THINK ABOUT AND DISCUSS

1. Why do you think God allowed his people to become slaves to Pharaoh? Why do you think he allows difficult situations into the lives of those whom he loves?

2. What is the explanation for Exodus 1:12, which tells us that the more the Egyptians were oppressed, the more they multiplied? In what ways may God bring good out of evil?

3. What does the incident with the midwives have to say to us about current debates over abortion?

2 Covenant Promises

(2:1-6:30)

The Book of Exodus is focused very much on the man, Moses, whose name appears frequently throughout the Bible. Who was he? Where did he come from? Why did God choose him? What made him special?

God always has the right man in the right place at the right time. We are now about to be introduced to him. God's man is Moses, born a slave but raised a prince. His sense of timing needs to correspond to God's timing, however; not until he is eighty will he be ready to do what God wants him to do....

What the princess saw (2:1-10)

Into the context of births and deaths come Moses' parents. They are not named until the genealogy of Moses and his brother, Aaron, is given in chapter 6. Moses' father is called Amram, a descendant of Levi. He married his aunt, his father's sister, Jochebed (6:20), in one of these relationships which God would later condemn (Lev. 18:12). Yet, although there was sin here, grace was working all the more, in order to preserve the future leader and redeemer of Israel alive.

Amram and Jochebed did not obey Pharaoh's command. They kept Moses safe as long as they could, then made special provision for him, by constructing a watertight device that could hide Moses among the bulrushes of the Nile. All the time, Miriam, his daughter, kept watch on the basket in which her brother lay.

One day, the princess came to bathe and found the basket. On discovering Moses, she recognized what was going on, but, in response to Miriam's request, was willing that Moses should be brought up under her guardianship, nursed by his own mother.

There was *faith* here, which Moses' parents exercised in God, believing that he was able to work out all things for them. It was faith that was *tested* by Pharaoh's decree; how long these days seemed! In one sense, it was easy to have faith when Moses could be seen and protected at home, but it was something else to commit him to God's care and the waters of the Nile! Yet God gave grace for this trial.

And what a remarkable *providence* it was that brought Pharaoh's daughter to the very spot where Moses lay in the basket. God's timing and his methods are all exactly right. In what way but this might it have been possible for Moses' own mother to bring him up? And who would have thought that the redeemer of God's people would have been nurtured and trained in the palace of the very king who was trying to oppress them!

What Moses saw (2:11-22)

Suddenly the story jumps forty years. 2:11 says that 'Moses had grown up', but Acts 7:23 supplies the age. Again there is a parallel with the way in which the story of Jesus is told us in the Gospels: apart from one reference to Jesus when he was twelve years old (Luke 2:41ff), we know nothing about Jesus until he appears as an adult at the age of thirty, to commence his public ministry.

During these years, Moses has learned the ways of the Egyptians, and he has learned the history of his own people. Little wonder, then, that the sight of an Egyptian beating a Hebrew angered him. With no one around to see, Moses murders the Egyptian and hides his body. Trying to reconcile two argumentative Hebrews the following day, he is shocked to be asked by one of them, 'Do you mean to kill me as you killed the Egyptian?'

> Moses rashly thinks he can deliver his people—God's people—in his own strength and at his own time. Instead, he has to learn to become a mere instrument of redemption in God's hand, and to wait for God's time.

Moses knows he must leave immediately. In God's providence, he goes to Midian, and stays with the priest of Midian, one of whose daughters, Zipporah, becomes his wife.

Having been saved from Pharaoh, Moses must now be saved from himself! He rashly thinks he can deliver his people—God's people—in his own strength and at his own time. Instead, he has to learn to become a mere instrument of redemption in God's hand, and to wait for God's time. Another forty years will pass before God's agenda allows Moses to do the work for which God has set him apart. So God empties Moses, and brings him to the realization that Egypt is not for him: 'I have been a sojourner in a foreign land', is the meaning of the name he gives his son, Gershom (2:22). 'Egypt is not my home, I'm just a-passing through…'.

What God saw (2:23-25)

All the time that Moses was gone from Egypt, the people of God were groaning under their load. The Pharaoh died, and Israel cried. Was there anyone capable of hearing them?

Well, yes—'God heard their groaning' (2:24). His ears are open to the cries of his people (Ps. 102:20). This is one of the Bible's great *anthropomorphisms*—a figure of speech in which God, although he has no physical body, is described in human and physical terms. He is spirit, yet has an ear (Isa. 59:1). This is language used in the Bible and by God to reveal himself to us, as a personal God, one who is not ignorant of our situation and our need.

More glorious, however, than the hearing of the groan is the fact that God 'remembered his covenant'. The promises he had made to the patriarchs, Abraham, Isaac and Jacob, were the foundation upon which God's intervention on behalf of his people would be built.

What is a covenant? It is a formal bond that ties two people, or two nations—any two parties—together. Perhaps the best illustration of a covenant is a marriage union. Two people fall in love and want to spend their lives with each other. There is a deep, personal attachment between them. In a sense, nothing can add to, or take away from that relationship. But it is important to guard the personal relationship with a formal, binding commitment—which is what marriage is. Once a couple is married, the relationship is different. The love and personal commitment are the same, but it now operates within the security of a public commitment. The marriage commitment is there simply to allow the personal love to grow and develop.

In the same way, God has bound himself in covenant to his people. He loves his people—he has a personal attachment to them. But he has formalized that attachment by making a public pledge to them. This is how he describes the covenant to Abraham:

> I will establish my covenant between me and you and your offspring after you throughout their generations for an everlasting covenant, to be God to you and to your offspring after you. And I will give to you and to your offspring after you the land of your sojournings, all the land of Canaan for an everlasting possession, and I will be their God (Genesis 17:7-8).

Here is God, pledging himself to be the God of his people, and committing himself to them. That theme runs through the Bible. Jesus is called the 'mediator of a new covenant' (Heb. 12:24), the one in whom God's pledge to his people is secure. Arguably, God's covenant with his people is the theme of the Bible. It is certainly the theme that runs through Exodus, as God acts in history to fulfil the promises he made to Abraham, Isaac and Jacob.

So God is a personal God, one who is aware of the needs of his people, and one who is committed to the promises he has made to them. Thus the foundation is laid in Exodus for the covenantal structure and unity of the Bible; here is one of the foundational terms which are so important for our understanding of the gospel.

Commissioning a Saviour (3:1-22)

God is now going to set his rescue plan in motion. His people are groaning. Moses is ready. The covenant is beckoning him to fulfil all that he purposed and promised to do for his people. The time has come for God to call Moses to the work that will be the means of leading the children of Israel out of the land of Egypt.

His call to Moses is quite wonderful. While Moses is going about his business as a shepherd, suddenly he is aware of a bush burning. Not an unusual sight, perhaps; but the fire seemed to be going on for a long time, and the bush was not being consumed by it.

What was the significance of the burning bush?

Some have suggested that it represented the situation of Israel in Egypt: like the bush, the people of God were enveloped in the flames of hardship, cruelty and oppression, yet they were not consumed. God was keeping his people alive.

Others have suggested that what we have here is a revelation of the brilliant, burning glory of God. The image of fire conveys the idea of purity, holiness, power and majesty.

The Puritan John Owen nuances this, however, and suggests that God was giving Moses an early symbol, or type, of the one whom he himself prefigured, the Lord Jesus Christ. This is how Owen puts it: 'The eternal fire of the divine nature dwells in the bush of our frail nature, yet is it not consumed thereby. God thus dwells in this bush, with all his goodwill towards sinners'.[6]

> God...remains the God of his people. His eye is on them, his ear has heard their cry, and his heart is towards them.

Each of these interpretations has merit, although given the language God uses in this passage, we should perhaps rule out the first. In some sense, God uses this burning bush to reveal something about his own character and glory, and the glory of his unchanging, mediated salvation which remains the hope and encouragement of those who are in slavery and bondage.

He is the God who knows the needs of his people.

Israel has not been forgotten by God. As he promised to Abraham, Isaac and Jacob (see how this formula from 2:24 is used in verse 6 and repeated in verses 15 and 16), he remains the God of his people. His eye is on them, his ear has heard their cry, and his heart is towards them (v. 7). In Egypt, in sin, in difficulties of all kinds, God is aware of what his people need.

He is the God who breaks in to save his people.

'I have come down to deliver them,' he says in verse 8, and to bring them to a better land. He will not leave his people where he found them, nor as he found them, but will intervene for their salvation. He did this in Egypt, but supremely in the Incarnation, when 'the Word became flesh and dwelt among us' (John 1:14).

He is the God who does not change.

Just as our attention was drawn to the significance of Moses' name (2:10), so now our attention is drawn to God's name. He is the great 'I am' (the Hebrew form of which gives us the name 'Jehovah'). He remains the same, and his covenant promises stand in spite of all the opposition of Egypt.

He is the God who authenticates his words with powerful signs.

God promises Moses that he will 'strike Egypt with all the wonders that I will do in it' (v. 20). That is the function of miracles in the Bible: to show the reality of the words of God's servants, culminating with Jesus himself. It is important to note that miracles appear sparingly in the Bible, and are always used for the purpose of showing that God's messengers have his commission and his approval.

Excuses, excuses (4:1-17)

Moses is reluctant to obey; in fact, he can think of several reasons why he should not.

FIRST, he argues that the Egyptians will not accept his claim to be a spokesman for God. So God shows his power: Moses' staff becomes a snake, his hand becomes leprous, and is then healed. In all of this, God is demonstrating his power, and reminding Moses of the strength of God's hand.

SECOND, he argues that he is no speaker (v. 10). Against this,

God counter-argues that he has made man's mouth, and promises that he will fill it with suitable and appropriate words.

FINALLY, Moses says: 'send someone else'. Although God is angry with Moses, he reminds him that his brother Aaron can speak well, and both of them will be spokesmen on behalf of God before Pharaoh.

Back to Egypt (4:18-31)

So finally, having graduated from Desert University at the age of eighty, Moses is ready to return to Egypt and to challenge Pharaoh to release God's people. Two important elements feed into the story on the way.

The first is the intimation of God's divine judgement against Pharaoh: 'I will harden his heart, so that he will not let the people go' (4:21). In spite of miracles and threats of judgement, Pharaoh's heart and mind will not bend to the things of God. But who hardens Pharaoh's heart? Is it God, as this verse (and other verses—7:3,13, 9:12, 10:20, 14:4) seems to suggest? Or is it Pharaoh himself, as 7:14, 22 and 9:34 seem to suggest?

The answer is—both. God's solemn, sovereign judgement on Pharaoh is simply that he will leave Pharaoh to his own devices, to the sinfulness and rebellion of his own heart. Moses is made aware of God's judgement on Pharaoh; but the responsibility for his refusal to obey is Pharaoh's own. Just as, in a later generation, it was God's sovereign purpose that Jesus should die, so those who crucified him had to bear responsibility for it. There is no contradiction between God's sovereignty and our responsibility.

The second thing that takes place here is the action of Zipporah, Moses' wife, who circumcised her son, and touched Moses' feet with the foreskin. The reason was that God threatened to kill Moses (4:24). The incident seems bizarre. We have already noted the repeated use of the formula 'the God of Abraham'; one of the main elements of the covenant with Abraham was the requirement that all the male descendants of Abraham be circumcised. Perhaps, therefore, God was bringing home to Moses his need to be absolutely obedient to all aspects of God's will if he was to be a suitable mediator, redeemer and saviour.

From bad to worse (5:1-23)

Following the confrontation with Pharaoh, however, in which God's message is faithfully delivered, things only get worse for God's people. Now they are to make bricks without straw (5:7). Their situation worsens, and does not improve.

> God's promise to deliver his people seems to be contradicted by the providences that have led to their situation being drastically made worse.

The result is that the Israelites grumble against Moses, blaming him and Aaron for making Israel repulsive to the Egyptians (5:21), who have made their situation so much more intolerable. This is probably what Pharaoh planned: he will not accede to Moses' request, so he will now drive a wedge between Moses and the very people he wishes to save.

Moses can only leave his case with God, asking him why he sent him to Pharaoh (5:22-23). God's promise to deliver his people seems to be contradicted by the providences that have led to their situation being drastically made worse.

Perhaps Moses still has a lot to learn. The desert taught him much, but experience can teach him more. He must learn to be still, and wait on God, relying wholly on the sovereign purpose of God which will ensure that the redemption of his people will take place.

Back to the covenant (6:1-13)

It is precisely in order to reassure Moses of this fact that God reminds Moses, and reminds us, once again that he is in the business of fulfilling covenant promises and undertakings. Once again we are brought back to Abraham, Isaac and Jacob, and to the covenant language that gives God's people the assurance that he is theirs and that they are his.

In spite of the fact that the Israelites were in no mood to listen to a sermon on the covenant (6:9), and in spite of the fact that Moses' reason tells him that if *Israel* won't listen to him, what hope is there that *Pharaoh* will (6:12), the covenant is the only source of hope and confidence that Moses has. It remains the case, throughout the whole history of the Book of Exodus, that God is at work to fulfil the promises which he covenanted to his people. And in the same way, we too are to place our trust in God's promises to us.

Getting things in perspective (6:14-30)

The genealogy of Moses and Aaron is inserted to give us an historical perspective on what God is doing. There are several interesting features of this genealogy.

FIRST, the genealogy reminds us of the continuity of the story of God's redeeming purpose. Egypt has not obliterated the identity of the people of God. They are descended from Jacob, and are important to God for that reason.

SECOND, there is the reminder that Moses and Aaron are descendants of Levi (6:16). That fact will become important later, when God will ordain that the priesthood will belong to the tribe of Levi. At this point, the significance of Levi is not so apparent, but we will be alerted to the fact that God's great work of salvation is not simply a *covenant* work, but a *priestly* work.

THIRDLY, the writer wishes to secure the identity of Moses and Aaron: 'These are the Aaron and Moses to whom the LORD said: "Bring out the people of Israel…"' (6:26). Aaron is the elder of the brothers, and is mentioned first; the genealogy serves to underscore the fact that this is genuine history.

For further study ▶

FOR FURTHER STUDY

1. Read Hebrews 11:23. In what ways was the faith of Moses' parents in evidence when they did what they did to preserve his life? What lessons may be learned from the parallel case of Jesus (Matt. 2:13-15), whose life in infancy was also threatened and miraculously preserved?

2. Read Acts 7:23-25. Stephen appears to give the impression that when Moses struck the Egyptian, he already knew that God was commissioning him to deliver God's people. Does that affect your reading of the Exodus story?

3. Does the Acts 7 comment suggest that Moses was trying to do God's work his own way?

4. Read Acts 7:26. Does this suggest that Moses tried to reconcile the two Hebrews first?

5. Exodus 2:24 talks about one covenant which God made with Abraham, Isaac and Jacob, rather than three covenants. What does this tell us about the unity of God's purpose in the Bible?

6. God's covenant with the patriarchs is further mentioned in Exodus 32:13 and 33:1. What additional information is conveyed in these passages?

7. Paul talks in Romans 9:18 about God 'hardening' people's hearts, just as he did with Pharaoh in the Book of Exodus. Why does Paul refer to this? What can we learn from Romans 9 about the relationship between God's sovereignty and the preaching of the gospel?

8. Jesus uses the phrase 'I Am', which is so central to the revelation of God's glory in Exodus 3, in John 8:58. What should we conclude from this about the relation of Jesus Christ to the God of the Old Testament?

1. What does the rescue of Moses tell us about the way God carries out his purposes and plans? Do you believe in coincidences?

2. Can the action of Moses in slaying the Egyptian be justified? What does *this* incident tell us about the way God overrules our faults to fulfil his purposes?

3. What was God doing when he brought Moses to the point of feeling like a stranger and all alone (Exod 2:22)?

4. What is the meaning of a covenant (Exod 2:24)?

5. How does the description of God 'hearing' and 'remembering' help us to understand what God is like?

6. 'There are not therefore two covenants of grace differing in substance, but one and the same under various dispensations' (Westminster Confession of Faith, 7.6). Do you agree with this statement?

7. What parallels can you find between the experience of Moses' call and commission in Exodus 3, and that of Jesus at his baptism in Matthew 3:13-17? What can we learn from these passages about the way(s) God calls people into his service?

8. How should the doctrine of God's sovereignty be preached? Are men and women excusable if God is the one who opens and who hardens the hearts of people?

9. Do you agree that miracles are performed only at certain points along the Bible's timeline, in order to authenticate God's divinely appointed messengers? If so, should the church today perform miracles?

3 Covenant Power

(7:1-12:32)

God is going to act in history for the redemption and salvation of his people. There will be opposition, but God's power is as good as his promise. As he reveals himself in word and action, he will break the chains that hold his people in bondage.

The time has now come for the word of God to be presented to Pharaoh alongside the revelation of God's power. Moses will be the means through which supernatural events will take place; these will culminate in the release of God's people, while at the same time confirming Pharaoh in his hardness, rebellion and wilful sin against God.

Challenging Pharaoh (7:1-13)

God compares Moses and Aaron to a god and his prophet before Pharaoh. Moses will communicate God's word, with Aaron further explaining the meaning and implications of the message. Again, God declares that he will harden Pharaoh's heart (7:3). So, at the respective ages of 80 and 83, Moses and Aaron go into the presence of Pharaoh.

It is important to note in this section the emphasis on God's activity: '*I* have made you like God' (v. 1); '*I* will harden Pharaoh's heart' (v. 3); '*I* will lay my hand on Egypt' (v. 4); 'when *I* stretch out my hand against Egypt and bring out the people of Israel' (v. 5). Although Moses and Aaron are God's chosen representatives and spokesmen, the activity and the work is clearly said to be God's. He is sovereignly working out his purpose to save and redeem his own.

A miracle is performed in the presence of Pharaoh, in which Aaron's rod becomes a serpent. Strangely, the magicians of Egypt can do the same thing. But their powerlessness is apparent when Aaron's rods swallow theirs. The battle here is a spiritual one, but God gives an indication that his power is greater than that of all the gods of Egypt.

Signs and Wonders (7:14-10:29)

The plagues that came on the land of Egypt represent a substantial part of the historical narrative and the biblical material. These are judgements which God sent on the land prior to the ultimate judgement which was to secure the release of his people.

The plagues were in the following order:

BLOOD (7:14-25)—in which the rivers of Egypt turn crimson red, and Pharaoh's heart is all the more hardened against God (7:22);

FROGS (8:1-15)—in which the land is covered by frogs,

swarming over every room and building. Pharaoh begs for respite and promises to free the people (8:8), but when the relief comes, his heart is hardened all the more (8:15);

GNATS (8:16-19)—in which the dust of the earth becomes gnats; the magicians recognize the handwork of God, but Pharaoh hardens against God (8:19);

FLIES (8:20-32)—in which swarms of flies cover the land. Pharaoh seems to relent (8:28), but once again hardens his heart (8:32);

LIVESTOCK (9:1-7)—in which a plague comes on the livestock, so that horses, cattle, sheep and other animals die. Again, Pharaoh is stubborn and hardens his heart (9:7);

BOILS (9:8-12)—in which men and beasts are covered with boils. Pharaoh's heart still refuses to yield (9:12);

HAIL (9:13-35)—in which heavy hailstones fall throughout the land of Egypt, with thunderstorms and lightning. The falls were so severe that trees fell (9:25). Pharaoh seems to acknowledge his sin (9:27), but once again, when he has relief from the hardship of the hail, he does not listen and hardens his heart (9:35);

LOCUSTS (10:1-20)—in which locusts cover every square inch of ground, devouring the trees and filling the houses. The effect on Pharaoh is the same (10:20);

DARKNESS (10:21-29)—in which a supernatural darkness descends on the land, making it impossible for people to see one another. Pharaoh bargains, but when the danger is passed, is still stubborn in his rebellion (10:27).

What is the explanation for these plagues?

Can these plagues be explained in terms of natural

phenomena? Some have suggested cosmic reasons, such as a meteor making contact with the earth; others have suggested seasonal reasons, beginning with the high water level of the River Nile; others have suggested geological reasons, perhaps with volcanic activity starting the whole process.7 It is possible to discern a naturalistic order in the plagues; if, for example, the rivers turned to blood, it is possible that this would result in frogs coming out of the water on to the land, resulting in flies swarming all over the place, producing boils and causing death.

However, this cannot explain all the plagues. Why should there be a shower of hail, or a thick darkness? Our key into explaining these phenomena is in the use of the phrase 'signs and wonders'; however much God harnessed the resources of nature, this was still a supernatural series of occurrences.

What was the reason for the plagues?

God draws our attention to at least three reasons for these plagues. The first was *to demonstrate his own power*. As a result of them, the people would know that he alone was God, and that he was going to show his superiority over all the gods of Egypt (12:12). Indeed, God says that this was the purpose for which he raised up Moses: 'to show you my power, so that my name may be proclaimed in all the earth' (9:16). With each plague, there came an increasing demonstration of the omnipotence of God.

A second reason was that God would *distinguish between the Egyptians and his people, the Israelites*. In 8:23 he gives this as an explanation why there would be no swarms of flies in Goshen, where his people lived: 'I will put a division between my people and your people.' That is evident in the plagues; for example, when darkness covers the land, 'all the people of Israel had light where they lived' (10:23). This was a judgement on Egypt, and with it, God distinguished between those who were his, and those who were not.

Finally, the plagues were a means for *hardening the heart of Pharaoh*. This is clear, for example, in 10:1, where God says to Moses that the signs he has worked among them have resulted in Pharaoh's further rebellion. God's power and works are no guarantee of compliance and obedience; in Pharaoh's case, they work the very opposite.

The ultimate threat (11:1-10)

Nine times God has demonstrated his power over Egypt, and on nine occasions Pharaoh has refused to let God's people go. So the time has come for God to act decisively and definitively. In fact, as far back as chapter 4, the threat of the death of the firstborn was in the background, as well as the reason for it: 'Then you shall say to Pharaoh, "Thus says the LORD, Israel is my firstborn son, and I say to you, 'Let my son go that he may serve me'. If you refuse to let him go, behold, I will kill your firstborn son"' (4:22-23).

In other words, the threat now to bring the last plague on Egypt, in which midnight would see the death of the firstborn in every Egyptian home, was to reflect the important place Israel had as the firstborn of God. No home was to be exempt; Pharaoh would suffer, and his slaves and prisoners would also suffer. Even the firstborn among the animals would die.

The Passover (12:1-28)

The events of Exodus 12 were so important that God draws up a new religious calendar beginning with the commemoration of Israel's redemption. The chapter is important not only because of the account of the redemption of Israel, but also because of the inauguration of the Festival of Passover. The first month of the year, the month Abib, or Nisan, was to be an important month, looking back to the definitive events of the exodus proper. This was when God led his people out. There are some important themes and issues in this chapter, the two most important being the Blood redemption and the Passover inauguration.

> God's people were spared the judgement which came upon the land of Egypt. But they were spared the death of the firstborn only through the death of a substitute: a lamb was to be slain, and its blood sprinkled on the door of their home.

The death of the substitutionary lamb

God's people were spared the judgement which came upon the land of Egypt. But they were spared the death of the firstborn only through the death of a substitute: a lamb was to be slain, and its blood sprinkled on the door of their home. Death came to every home in Egypt: either the death of the firstborn, or the death of the lamb.

Not just any lamb could be slain for the purpose of

redemption. The lamb had to be 'without blemish, a male a year old' (12:5); that is, in the best condition from either the sheep or the goats. Each household had to shelter under the blood of the lamb, or perish. The application of the death of the lamb was twofold: the blood of redemption and atonement was applied to the homes, and the flesh of the lamb was eaten. In these ways, everyone had a personal interest in the lamb which was slain on their behalf.

Yet the blood of the passover lamb was not only (and perhaps not primarily) a sign for Israel, but for God! God says: 'when *I* see the blood I will pass over you...' (12:13). This idea of passing over is what gives the commemorative feast its name. God's satisfaction with the death of the lamb is expressed in this way; his justice is satisfied, and his honour vindicated.

The inauguration of the Passover ceremony

The eating of the lamb on the night of Israel's redemption was to follow a detailed pattern, and was to be accompanied with unleavened bread and with bitter herbs. It was to be eaten by people who were ready to leave at a moment's notice, and anything left over in the morning had to be burned (12:10, 11).

God requires his people to hold an annual commemorative feast which will be a 'memorial' of the great deliverance from Egypt. This chapter, therefore, functions not only as an account of the redemption, but also as an explanation for the Passover meal, which was to be part of the feast of Unleavened Bread, an annual, seven-day festival in which leaven, or yeast, was removed out of the house (12:15), the people were to gather in holy assembly, and were to keep the festival of redemption. Later in the history of Israel, this feast was not observed privately, but as part of the tabernacle and Temple ritual (see Deut. 16:5-7).

In his commentary on Exodus, Professor John L Mackay observes that 'the description of the Passover meal in Exodus 12 has some striking resemblances to the ritual followed in chapter 29 when Aaron and his sons were consecrated as priests'[8]. These included the slaughter of a ram, the sprinkling of the blood, and the eating of the flesh along with unleavened bread. Passover therefore functioned not only as a means of redemption *from* Egypt, but also as a sign of consecration *to* God.

The death of the firstborn (12:29-32)

Finally the solemn judgement falls on Egypt at midnight, just as God had forewarned. Every house was affected. Now Pharaoh's heart bends to the divine, sovereign, solemn moment, and he summons Moses, urging him to hasten the departure of Israel out of Egypt. God is not mocked (Gal. 6:7); his word is fulfilled, and his threat is carried out.

For further study ▶

FOR FURTHER STUDY

1. Compare Exodus 7:20 with John 2:9—the first miracles of Moses and Jesus respectively. What do these passages suggest about the comparisons and contrasts between Moses and Jesus?

2. Look at the following verses: Nehemiah 1:10, Psalm 107:2, Isaiah 62:12, Jeremiah 31:11. What word is common to them? How are God's people characterized in the Bible?

3. Read Matthew 26:17-29. Jesus wants to keep the Passover, but he inaugurates a new rite, which we call the Lord's Supper. What are the similarities between Passover and Lord's Supper? What are the differences? What does this passage tell us about the continuity between the Old and New Testaments?

4. In 1 Corinthians 5:7, Jesus is described as 'Christ our Passover Lamb'. What other references are there in the New Testament to Jesus as the Lamb? How does Exodus shed light for us on the work of Jesus for us?

TO THINK ABOUT AND DISCUSS

1. In spite of threats and warnings, Pharaoh refuses to listen to the voice of God. He sees many wonderful things, but is not obedient. Compare this with the effect of Christ's miracles in John 12:37, and its implications for the extent to which sin has affected our understanding and will.

2. Jesus uses the picture of leaven, or yeast, to describe the sin of hypocrisy (Luke 12:1). What sins does Paul compare to leaven in 1 Corinthians 5:8? What leaven do you need to put out of your life? What leaven can damage the witness of the church?

3. The theme of redemption is a common one in modern hymns. What difference should it make in our lives to be able to sing that we are 'redeemed by the blood of the lamb'?

PART 2

Travelling the King's Highway

4 God opens a way

(12:33-14:31)

The God of Israel proves himself to be greater than all the gods of Egypt. Although the Israelites were slaves, the events of the exodus show that it is the Egyptians who are in spiritual bondage. God is going to show us that those whom he sets free are free indeed!

It seems almost too good to be true, but now, four centuries after coming to Egypt, the descendants of Jacob are finally on their journey out of Egypt to the land which God has promised to give them to inherit. This is their journey of a lifetime. God has opened a door for them; and walking through it is just the beginning of the adventure.

Leaving Egypt (12:33-42)

This important summary passage enables us to keep our perspective on what the exodus means for God's people.

FIRST, it meant victory over the Egyptians. It is interesting to note how the language of *warfare* is used to describe the people of God as they leave the land of their captors. It was as an army ready for battle that they left Egypt (13:18), and like an army who had plundered their foes (12:36). So eager were the Egyptians to see Israel leave that they paid them to go, giving them silver, gold and clothing. This is important because it explains how they have sufficient material later for constructing the tabernacle. But it also shows us who the real captives were in this conflict; not the children of Israel, to whom God restored all that Egypt had taken from them (*cf* the same sentiment in Ps. 69:4 AV and Joel 2:25), but the Egyptians, from whom Israel took so much.

SECOND, it meant freedom for thousands of Israelites. The number of 600,000 men is given in 12:37, which does not include women and children.[9] In addition, others went with them, as well as cattle and herds (12:38). The result was spectacular: 430 years of dwelling in Egypt had come to an end through the supernatural intervention of God. No wonder this was a night worth remembering and keeping as a memorial to the Lord (12:42).

Passover (12:43-51)

Another reference to the Passover in this summary context reminds us of the importance of this festival as commemorating the events described here. In this passage, however, detailed stipulations are given as to who may participate in the festival. Foreigners and 'hired servants' are excluded, while 'all the congregation of Israel' are included. This includes those who willingly join themselves to the covenant community through circumcision (12:48).

Already we are being alerted to a point which will be further developed in connection with the tabernacle and its construction and worship: that God must regulate his own worship. He outlines the reason for observing the Passover—because he himself 'kept watch' over his people (12:42). He can exclude or include, he can excommunicate and can also determine who may participate. Neither the people nor their leaders were given the authority to make these regulations; theirs was a call to total obedience to the Lord, who alone can stipulate the nature of his own worship.

Consecrated to the Lord (13:1-16)

The reference to the firstborn in 13:2 is another important link in the unfolding of this narrative. Israel was God's firstborn (4:22); God struck Egypt's firstborn, and now he claims the firstborn of Israel's families and flocks to belong to him.

The consecration of the firstborn was a reflection, once again, of the total commitment of the people to the God who had redeemed them. The relation between redemption and consecration—between salvation and holiness—is explained in the passage that follows, in which the redemption from Egypt and the rituals surrounding the Passover are in the foreground.

The Feast of Unleavened Bread, which culminated in the Passover meal, was to be kept annually by God's people. Furthermore, each generation was to pass on both the feast and the explanation for it to the next generation (13:8), and each occasion of observance was a further sign of God's graciousness to them in the past.

But there is always a close link between past and present, between redemption accomplished and consecration required. That is why the Passover is described not merely as a memorial of the past, but a sign that 'the law of the Lord may be in your mouth' (13:9). In other words, each time an Israelite participated in the Feast, he was pledging his commitment to keep God's law, and not just remembering the events which shaped his people and their faith.

This is then further elaborated in the regulations governing the firstborn (13:11-16). Commitment to the Lord is to be signalled by the redemption of all those who 'open the womb', and will represent the devotion of all the people to the God of Israel.

The way-maker (13:17-22)

Looking at any map will show that there was a pretty much direct route from Egypt to Canaan, through the land of the Philistines. However, we are told here why God did not lead his people by that direct route. He took them by way of the Red Sea, in order to deepen their faith in him and ensure that it would not be shaken by the events which they would encounter, 'lest the people change their minds when they see war and return to Egypt' (13:17). They would face difficult challenges, hostile foes and experiences of war. But the wilderness years would be years of formation, of development, of maturing and of learning.

The reference to Joseph's bones in 13:19 is important. Genesis closes with Joseph's charge to his brothers not to leave his bones in Egypt, but to have them buried in the promised land (see Gen. 50:25). Was this just sentiment? Or was there something deeper here? There is certainly something deeply moving about the thought of Moses carrying the bones of Joseph out of Egypt as Israel commenced their journey. In fact, Hebrews 11:22 draws our attention to this—'By faith Joseph, at the end of his life, made mention of the exodus of the Israelites and gave directions concerning his bones'. Joseph's commission was full of faith in God's promise, believing that Egypt was not the ultimate destination of God's people, but that he had a better place for them to dwell in.

The journey commences, with God leading his people in a fiery presence (remember that it was in a *burning* bush he had appeared to Moses), which gave the appearance of cloud during the day, but fire at night. This theme will be taken up again at the end of the Book of Exodus (40:34-38), but is important in this summary also. It is a reminder to us that the presence of God is a constant one; the God who redeems his people also promises to guide and protect his people.

The Red Sea (14:1-31)

Suddenly Pharoah awakens to the realization of what has happened—Israel has left Egypt! How could they have allowed this to happen? Pharaoh marshals his troops and pursues Israel with hardened heart in order to prevent them escaping.

This chapter juxtaposes God's sovereign judgement on Pharaoh ('I will harden Pharaoh's heart'—14:4) with Pharaoh's own wilful rebellion. For God's people, however, the danger soon becomes apparent, as they find themselves trapped between 'the devil and the deep Red Sea', between Pharaoh's armies and the Red Sea.

The Israelites are quick to cry out to Moses, and even against Moses. Has he led them out of Egypt only to have them perish in the wilderness? Would it not have been better for them simply to perish where they were, than fill them with false hopes which would be dashed so quickly?

Moses knows, however, that the people need to be reminded of the all-powerful nature of the God who keeps his promises. There are times for moving, and there are times for standing still. Even although the best forces of Pharaoh's army are closing in on them from behind, Moses tells them that this is a time to 'stand firm, and see the salvation of the LORD' (14:13), a time to realize that God would fight for them (14:14).

> Moses knows, however, that the people need to be reminded of the all-powerful nature of the God who keeps his promises. There are times for moving, and there are times for standing still.

Once again the word of Moses is authenticated with a display of awesome, divine power, as he raises his staff over the waters of the river, in response to the command of God. The people witness the diverging of the waters, as God makes a path through the sea which will allow his people to cross over. This is a second 'passover' experience, as they traverse the wide river, with God's presence standing 'between the host of Egypt and the host of Israel' (14:20), hiding his people and protecting them from their enemies.

Not only does Israel manage to cross on dry ground, but the Egyptians, who drive their chariots along the dry path through the Red Sea, suddenly find themselves submerged beneath the waves of the sea as God brings the wall of water crashing back down into its course. As the sun rises, the Egyptians have either perished or returned. The problem has been taken away. God has been true to his promise.

Throughout the narrative, the reason for this display of power is evident. 'I will get glory over Pharaoh,' says God in 14:4, 17 and 18. The greater glory belongs to Jehovah, who fights on behalf of his people. In turn, they have become witnesses of his power, which in turn has confirmed their faith in God and their trust in his spokesmen, Moses and Aaron (14:31).

FOR FURTHER STUDY

1. Read Exodus 13:1-16 again, and think about the relationship between redemption and consecration. How is this theme developed in the following passages: Isaiah 62:12, Ephesians 1:3-7, 1 Peter 1:13-18?

2. Look again at the references to Joseph's charge about his bones in Genesis 50:25, Exodus 13:19 and Hebrews 11:22. What do these references tell us about Joseph's faith and hope? What do they tell us about *our* faith and hope?

3. The presence of God in fire and cloud is an important theme of the Book of Exodus. Study the following references: Numbers 14:14, Deuteronomy 31:15, Nehemiah 9:12, 19, Psalm 99:7. Look up the following references to the presence of God with his people: Matthew 28:20, 2 Timothy 4:17, Hebrews 13:5. What can we conclude from these references about God's nearness to his people?

4. Hebrews 11:29 refers to the faith of Moses in connection with the crossing of the Red Sea. What other incidents in the life of Moses are referred to in Hebrews 11? How does faith help us in different circumstances?

TO THINK ABOUT AND DISCUSS

1. 1 Corinthians 11:23-29 lays down guidelines for celebrating the Lord's Supper. How do these compare with the guidelines for the Passover? Do the feasts shed light on each other?

2. Have there been situations in your life where you felt like the Israelites, trapped between Pharaoh and the Red Sea? Have there been times when God has stepped in to help you and to make his presence and power known? Discuss what these meant to you at the time.

3. The Israelites knew that God was with them because they saw a pillar that took on the appearance of a cloud, and of fire. How do we know that God is with us today?

5 God gives a song

(15:1-21)

Deliverance always leads to praise! God's people praise him because he has redeemed them; worthy of all praise as our Creator, he is especially to be worshipped as our Redeemer and Saviour.

The display of God's power and might, enabling Israel to cross the Red Sea, is celebrated in the song which Moses and the people sang. It is a vivid and unique celebration of what God did for them when they were powerless to do anything for themselves.

The song of Moses (15:1-21)

Several features of this song are worth noting.

FIRST, it *reveals some of the attributes of God*. In fact, this song is one of the most important pieces of explicit theology in the Scriptures. Let's note, in reverse order, some of the statements of the opening stanzas of the song. Moses tells about the *name* of God: the LORD is his name. Here there are clear echoes of chapter 3, where God revealed his name to Moses, and vindicated his character in the subsequent history of God's people.

Moses also tells us about the *character* of God. He is 'a man of war'. This does not contradict the Bible's statement that God is not a man (1 Sam. 15:29). Moses is using a powerful figure of speech, in which God is compared to a mighty warrior, engaged in battle against enemy forces. The reality is that God's people are not simply embroiled in a political conflict, but a deeply spiritual one. They can only overcome through the power of God assisting them.

Moses reminds us of the *covenant* nature of God. He describes him as 'my father's God' in verse 2. Just as God demonstrated his power and glory in the past, so he does now; nothing shows the reality of the unchanging God whose name is 'I am' quite like the historical record of his work for his people in every age and generation.

But the song begins on a supremely individual note, as Moses reminds us that God is his *personal* God, the one who enables him to sing, to exult and to praise. 'The LORD is *my* strength and *my* song,' he says, 'and he has become *my* salvation' (v. 2). That, at last, is the beauty of all God's great works and wonders in the Bible: they become personal to all those who experience his power and grace.

SECOND, it *gives an insight into the pride and folly of Pharaoh*. Look at how vividly this song portrays not only the collapse of Pharaoh's army in the depths of the sea (15:4-5), but how it builds up the picture of Pharaoh and his men scheming to overthrow God and his people, saying, 'I will pursue, I will overtake, I will divide the spoil, my desire shall have its fill of them. I will draw my sword, my hand shall destroy them' (15:9). One can almost hear the plans whirling round Pharaoh's head as the chariot wheels pummel the ground, gathering speed, recklessly chasing after the covenant people of God.

Yet all it takes is for God to blow with his wind (15:10), and the Egyptian armies are no more. All the plans of men and gods come to nothing when God acts in judgement over his enemies. 'Who is like you among the gods?' Moses asks, with words echoed in Psalms 86:8 and 89:6. The revelation we have here of God is of one who is without peer, who is incomparable and utterly unique.

THIRD, the song *highlights the purpose of God's salvation.* God is not acting arbitrarily in all of this; he is working out his sovereign purposes, leading out his people, in covenant love and mercy, according to his plan to guide them to his holy abode (15:13). And all the kings of the nations are pictured as standing silent and open-mouthed as God brings his purchased, redeemed Israel to the sanctuary he has established (15:17). He reigns eternally (15:18).

The song, therefore, is important within the context of Exodus as a theological reflection on who God is, what God has done, and what he has purposed to do for his redeemed people. And for that reason, it takes on added significance as John the Apostle hears God's people in heaven singing 'the song of Moses and of the Lamb' (Rev. 15:3), a song which is new, and yet which is as old as the exodus itself.

For further study ▶

FOR FURTHER STUDY

1. Read Psalms 78 and 136. How did the later Israelite tradition celebrate the crossing of the Red Sea?

2. There are other passages of Scripture that speak about God fighting on behalf of his people. Look, for example, at 2 Kings 6:17, Nehemiah 4:20, 1 John 4:4, Revelation 17:14. How does this help us to understand God? Or to understand the situation of his people in this world?

3. In spite of the fact that the Israelites crossed the Red Sea on dry land, 1 Corinthians 10:2 talks about Israel being in some sense 'baptized' in the sea. What do you think Paul means?

TO THINK ABOUT AND DISCUSS

1. We often talk about God's *attributes* and characteristics in impersonal terms; for example, we speak about his power, his wisdom, or his strength. Yet the Bible speaks in much more personal and concrete terms, such as in 15:3, 'the LORD is a man of war'. Which is more helpful? What other metaphors does the Bible use for God?

2. Why are the saints in heaven portrayed as singing the song of Moses (Rev. 15:3)?

3. Many of the Psalms celebrate God's redemptive works in history, a theme which is missing from many modern hymns. Why is it important to celebrate what God has done in the past?

6 God meets the need

(15:22-17:7)

God is not just the God of the new beginning—he is also the God of the entire pilgrimage of his people. As the journey unfolds, God's people will discover the riches of his grace and his provision for them. Having begun a new thing, he maintains it and continues it along the way.

You cannot take 600,000 men, as well as their wives and children, on a journey into the desert without coming across some basic hitches and snags to do with food and drink! Yet God continued to demonstrate his love, faithfulness, grace and power, by making provision for his people in the most remarkable of ways.

Bitter water made sweet (15:22-27)

After a journey of three days in the desert, water became a necessary commodity, but there was none. Imagine the delight of Israel to come across water; but imagine then

Israel's dismay when the water was discovered to be bitter and undrinkable! The name of the place was called 'Marah', meaning 'bitter', a Hebrew word which took on a powerfully personal significance in the Book of Ruth when Naomi (whose name meant 'pleasant'), asked that she be called 'Marah' because of the way in which God's hand had been against her.

> The 'testing' referred to is the challenge of giving total obedience to God; all along the way, God is looking for total commitment and consecration.

However, God was able to turn the bitter water into sweet, thirst-quenching water. God asked Moses to throw a log into the water, and it became sweet. The chapter adds the intriguing comment that 'there the LORD made for them a statute and a rule, and there he tested them.' In a sense, this was a preparation for the giving of the law at Sinai, which was also a place of testing.

The 'testing' referred to is the challenge of giving total obedience to God; all along the way, God is looking for total commitment and consecration. Will his people listen to his voice or not (Ps. 81:8ff)? The promise to those who will hear and obey him is that he will not allow them to be afflicted with the diseases that afflicted the Egyptians. The Lord may be a man of war, but he is also a healer (15:26).

That became evident when God eventually took his people to Elim, to the springs of water and the palm trees. What a contrast with Marah! Yet so often in the experience of God's people, their journeys take them to Marah today and Elim tomorrow; God always knows what is best for his people.

Bread from heaven (16:1-36)

The need for water was accompanied with a need for food. In spite of seeing how God can make provision in the most unpromising of circumstances, the Israelites continued to grumble and complain, accusing Moses of bringing them out to the wilderness only to kill them with hunger (16:3).

In fact, God's provision for his people at this point was to exceed their expectations. God promised that he would 'rain down' bread from heaven, and for forty years in the wilderness, he fed his people with manna (Ps. 78:24-25), and with quails, which was justification enough for Stephen's claim that Moses led them out of Egypt, 'performing signs and wonders in Egypt and at the Red Sea and in the wilderness for forty years' (Acts 7:36).

Several things about the manna are worth noting.

FIRST, this was a *supernatural* provision. There was nothing ordinary about this fare. Indeed, Psalm 78:25 describes it as the 'food of angels', a reference, no doubt, to the fact that God provided it for his people in an extraordinary way.

SECOND, it was a *daily* provision, yet it did not appear every day. God purposely tested his people to see if they would walk in his law (16:4) by sending manna for six days out of seven, with the promise of a double portion on the sixth day that would provide two days' food. The passage will later talk about the solemnity and holiness of the Sabbath day as the reason for this arrangement (16:23, 25, 26, 29).

This is extremely important, because by the time the Sabbath law is given at Sinai, the pattern of a weekly day of rest has already been established. The fourth commandment, while requiring that one day in seven be given to the Lord for worship, does not stipulate which day that should be. That must be established on other grounds, and is established, first, by the pattern of God's creation, and second, by the law regarding the manna.

There was a very practical implication to all of this. While the manna was available for all, it had to be gathered strictly according to God's regulations. Those who left the manna on the ground until the following day discovered that it had putrefied (16:20); on the other hand, those who gathered in the double portion on the sixth day found the portion for the seventh to be as fresh as any other. At the same time, any who went out on the Sabbath day for a fresh supply discovered there was none (16:26).

THIRD, it was a *sufficient* provision. In spite of the large number of people who needed food, God's supply was bountiful. It was one of the great miracles of the desert floor that there was always enough manna. There was neither too much nor too little (16:17-18). Families and individuals discovered that God's provision is always just enough.

FOURTH, it was a *constant* provision. Our attention is drawn to the fact that this supply remained the source of their nourishment for the duration of the wilderness journey: 'The people of Israel ate the manna forty years, till they came to a habitable land. They ate the manna till they came to the border of the land of Canaan' (16:35). This is further clarified and corroborated in the narrative of their entrance into Canaan, concerning which we read that God's people kept the Passover, 'and the day after the Passover, on that very day, they ate of the produce of the land, unleavened cakes and parched grain. And the manna ceased the day after they ate of the produce of the land. And there was no longer manna for the people of Israel, but they ate of the fruit of the land of Canaan that year' (Josh. 5:11-12). It was food for the wilderness, and the supply never stopped until God fulfilled his promise and took his people into the land of Canaan.

FIFTH, it was a provision to be held as a *memorial* to God's grace and goodness. This sweet tasting, heavenly bread was to be preserved in a jar before the presence of God (16:31-34). As such, it was to become one of several items relating to the Ark of the Covenant. Hebrews 9:4 says that the Ark contained the jar of manna, although 1 Kings 8:9 appears to contradict this. It is not unreasonable to suppose, however, that by the time the Ark is placed in the Temple, after it had been captured by the Philistines, the pot of manna may have been removed from it. Whatever the truth of the matter, the manna in the jar was kept before the Lord as a testimony to his goodness to his people.

> In spite of previous blessing, the people still find it easy to grumble and complain.

Water from the rock (17:1-7)

In spite of previous blessing, the people still find it easy to grumble and complain. Again, the grumbling has to do with water. As they come to Rephidim, the last stop before Sinai (see Num. 33:14-15), the people of Israel ask, 'Where will God find water for us, and how can he satisfy the needs of so many people in such a place as this?' For this reason, Rephidim becomes Massah, or Meribah, the place of testing (see Ps. 81:7).

Moses brings his burden to the Lord. While the people complain *against* God, Moses complains TO God. God commands Moses to strike the rock, from which water gushes out (17:6). Again, the supernatural nature of God's provision is evident to all Israel.

But it is interesting to see what the New Testament makes of this incident: Paul says of God's people that 'they all drank the same spiritual drink, for they drank from the spiritual Rock that followed them, and the Rock was Christ' (1 Cor. 10:4). In some sense, therefore, the striking of the rock at Rephidim, resulting in the provision of water, provides us with an analogy of the one who is our Rock, and who gives us spiritual water to drink: Jesus Christ himself.

FOR FURTHER STUDY

1. Why does Jesus refer to the manna in John 6:31-35? What similarities can we find between the provision of manna in the wilderness and the Bread of Life who is Jesus Christ?

2. Read Hebrews 9:1-5. Where is the manna discussed in this context? And why? In what sense can Paul identify the Rock from which Israel drank with Christ (1 Cor. 10:4)?

TO THINK ABOUT AND DISCUSS

1. Why do you think God's people were so ready to disbelieve his promise and doubt his provision? What are the things that ought to encourage us today in the belief that God will meet all our needs?

2. Just as God's people had to be fed daily on heavenly bread, so too must we. What parallels can you find between the regulations for the daily gathering of manna, and our need to walk closely with God and feed on him day by day?

3. Do you think the Sabbath principle ('Tomorrow is a day of solemn rest, a holy Sabbath to the LORD...' 16:23) is still valid for Christians today?

7 God helps a leader

(17:8-18:27)

It's easy to forget that the men God uses are—well—men! Like Elijah, described as 'a man with a nature like ours' (James 5:17), Moses is human, too. He has been the means of supernatural blessings, and through him God has done wonderful things. But here we catch a glimpse of the way God helps the men he uses.

The role of Moses has been clearly identified by God, as it is through him that God has communicated all his previous messages to Israel. But that role is now consolidated further, in the incident with Amalek, as well as in the aftermath of the battle.

Moses oversees a battle (17:8-16)

While they are still camped at Rephidim, the Amalekites fight against Israel. They are the first of the enemy armies to threaten Israel after Israel had left Egypt. Amalek was the grandson of Esau, Jacob's brother (Gen. 36:15-16), and therefore the personal hostility between Jacob (whom God called Israel) and his estranged brother Esau is perpetuated in their descendants, as the children of Amalek do battle with the children of Israel.

The image of the battle is an intriguing one. The narrative introduces us to Joshua, whom we meet at 17:10 for the first time. He is going to have an important role among God's people during their wilderness journey; he is going to succeed Moses as their leader and take them into the promised land; and he is to have a Bible book named after him. Yet we know virtually nothing about him at this point, simply that he is a first-rate swordsman, who goes into the battle against Amalek.

Meanwhile Moses, Aaron and Hur go to a mountain plateau from which they are able to survey the battle. While Moses' hands are raised, Israel prevails, but while his hands are lowered, Amalek prevails. No doubt the raised hands portray Moses as a suppliant and an intercessor (Ps. 141:2). Eventually Moses finds that his arms are heavy and sore, so Aaron and Hur hold up his hands while he himself sits down. Thus he was able to raise his hands until sunset, and Israel prevailed.

> It is as important that Joshua fights with the sword as that Moses should wrestle in prayer. Neither would be effective without the other.

The two actions, therefore, are important: it is as important that Joshua fights with the sword as that Moses should wrestle in prayer. Neither would be effective without the other. The battle does not depend ultimately on Joshua's skill as a swordsman; but neither is it won apart from Joshua's engagement. Similarly, Moses' prayer is nothing without the practical service of Joshua, who remains dependent on Moses' intercession, even although he cannot see him or hear him beyond the din of battle.

There are two consequences of this battle. First, Moses builds an altar to God, a place of worship which serves as a renewed point of confessing and acknowledging God to be the banner and the strength of his people (17:15). Second, Amalek comes under God's perpetual judgement, as he says, 'I will surely blot out the memory of Amalek from under heaven' (17:14). This latter point is so important that it is set before Israel again in Deuteronomy 25:17-19. Moses urges the people of God not to forget what Amalek did, and not to forget how God responded.

Moses shares the work (18:1-27)

The leadership of Moses is also the focus of interest in this chapter, although the context is much more personal. Indeed, our attention is drawn to Moses the family man, rather than to Moses the leader of Israel. In particular, the story revolves around Jethro, the father of Zipporah, and the father-in-law of Moses.

We cannot be sure when this account of Jethro's visit to Moses took place. Moses had evidently sent Zipporah and his two sons, Gershom and Eliezer, to the safety of Jethro's home, but there may be reason to suppose that the story does not follow chapter 17 in strict chronological order. For one reason, the very problem raised in chapter 18 seems to suggest a knowledge of the laws and the statutes given by God in later chapters. At any rate, our attention is immediately drawn to the fact that Jethro was a Midianite, and belonged to a tribe which, like Amalek, would prove to be hostile to Israel (see, for example, Judg. 6:3, which names both tribes among the enemies of Israel). Yet not all Canaanites were like Amalek, and not all Midianites were like Midian.

One of the first things to happen following Jethro's arrival was that Moses gave him a firsthand account of all that had happened up to this point. God had delivered his people out of Egypt (18:8), and Jethro rejoiced in this, confessing Jehovah to be the supreme God among all the gods.

Then, however, Jethro observed Moses, who, according to 18:13, 'sat to judge the people, and the people stood around Moses from morning till evening'. We might note in passing that this detail establishes Moses' role not merely as an administrator of justice, but as a king. The later judges of Israel fulfil a similar function, and the Bible seems to use the words 'king' and 'judge/ruler' interchangeably (as in Psalm 2:10). We are made aware, therefore, that as Moses fulfils priestly functions, as in his intercession during the battle with Amalek, so he fulfils kingly functions in governing the people.

Jethro is not impressed, however. Although Moses is an able administrator, he is only a man. The counsel Jethro gives him is plain, commonsense advice: '... the thing is too heavy for you,' he says, 'you are not able to do it alone ... look for able men from all the people, men who fear God ... it will be

> Moses, with his great responsibility to lead, is not averse to being led; with his great task of teaching, he is not unwilling to learn. We all need to learn such advice.

easier for you, and they will bear the burden with you' (18:18, 21, 22). Jethro's advice was that Moses should be left with major issues to settle, while lesser matters could easily be delegated to others to resolve. Moses took his advice.

This is an important passage, in which Moses, with his great responsibility to lead, is not averse to being led; with his great task of teaching, he is not unwilling to learn. We all need to learn such advice; perhaps the hundreds of thousands in Israel never knew what a help Jethro had been to them in the simple advice he gave his son-in-law about taking care of himself.

1. What other references can you find in the Bible to Amalek and the Amalekites? In particular, what does 1 Samuel 15:17-23 teach about the relationship between Amalek and God's later rejection of Saul as king?

2. In Exodus 17, Moses is portrayed as an intercessor, as one who prayed to God for the battle going on in the valley. What encouragement should we get from passages like Romans 8:34 or Hebrews 7:25 which talk of Jesus fulfilling this role for us?

3. Read Acts 6:1-6. What comparison can you find between Jethro's advice to Moses in Exodus 18, and the advice of the twelve apostles to the early church?

TO THINK ABOUT AND DISCUSS

1. What is the relationship between prayer and service? What lessons should we learn from the fact that as Joshua fought, Moses prayed? And what can we learn from Exodus 17 about the need to persevere in prayer?

2. Jethro was afraid that Moses would suffer from 'burnout' and exhaustion. How real a danger is this in our service for the Lord? How easy is it for you to spot danger signs? How ready are you to listen to good, practical advice?

76

PART 3

Experiencing the King's Presence

8 Meeting the King

(19:1-20:21)

The glory of God is one of the recurring themes of Exodus. At this point of the narrative, God's glory is going to be displayed once again in the desert of Sinai, at Mount Horeb. He is going to come down among his people, and is going to communicate with them in an unprecedented way.

It is important to remember that when God commissioned Moses to lead his people out of Egypt, he gave him a promise: 'I will be with you, and this shall be the sign for you, that I have sent you: when you have brought the people out of Egypt, you shall serve God on this mountain' (3:12). The second part of that promise is about to be fulfilled as God's people come to Sinai, or Horeb, to the very spot where God had revealed himself to Moses, and where now he is to reveal himself spectacularly and powerfully to his people.

At Mount Sinai (19:1-25)

The arrival at Sinai is heralded with an important introductory statement: 'On the third new moon after the people of Israel had gone out of the land of Egypt, on that day they came into the wilderness of Sinai' (19:1). In other words, the theophany ('appearance of God') at Sinai took place about seven weeks after the Passover-redemption from Egypt. This timeframe is reflected in later Old Testament legislation governing the feasts of Israel (e.g. Lev. 23:16), and in the New Testament, in which the coming of the Holy Spirit at Pentecost takes place about seven weeks after the death of Jesus Christ.

God's preliminary word to Israel is a reminder of the special and privileged place Israel has in the purposes of God. They have been redeemed by him, have been carried by him, and are regarded as a unique treasure by him among all the nations of the world. That blessing is unconditional in the sense that it is all of his own marvellous grace; but it is conditional in the sense that it requires of them that they keep his covenant (19:5).

Important also is the language of God's *coming* to his people: 'Behold I am coming to you in a thick cloud,' he says in 19:9. This theme is important in Exodus. Just as God came to visit his people in their affliction in Egypt (3:8), so now he is going to come down in a special way to reveal his covenant law to them.

19:9-15 details the preparation required for the people to be ready for the advent of their King. Just as Moses discovered in chapter 3, the place where God reveals himself is a holy place; as Moses could not come near to the burning bush (3:5), so the people must remain at a distance from the mountain (19:12). Just as the bush burned with flame (3:2), so God would descend on Sinai in fire (19:18). And just as Moses was afraid to look at God (3:6), so the people tremble before the theophany (19:16). All of this requires of them that they consecrate themselves, symbolized by washing their clothes and abstaining from sexual intercourse.

Then, on the third day, the Lord was present among his people. Sinai was wrapped in smoke, thus relating the presence of God in the pillar of cloud with his presence on Mount Sinai. The appearance of God is heralded by the blast of a trumpet and by thunder and lightning. Only Moses may approach God; everyone else must stay away, for fear that they be consumed by the glory of God.

The Ten Commandments (20:1-21)

Before looking at the Ten Commandments, it is important to take a more general look at the whole question of law, and its relationship to covenant. We have already noted that God redeemed his people because he remembered his covenant with them (2:24), and he gives his law to them so that they will keep his covenant (19:5). The idea of covenant is bigger than the idea of law. Yet the Book of Exodus describes the law of God as the 'book of the covenant' (Exod. 24:7). So what is the relationship between covenant and law? That question may be answered in various ways.

FIRST, *the law reveals the nature of the God of the covenant.* As God penned the rules which his people were to obey, he was revealing to them some of his own characteristics. He is a God of holiness, of majesty, of justice, of sovereignty. As he gives the law to his people he says, 'I am the LORD your God' (Exod. 20:2), covenant words which remind his people of the majesty that belongs to him.

SECOND, *the law defines the people of the covenant.* The regulations for living which God gave to his people made them distinctive. They were devoted to Jehovah. God was setting them apart. 'Keeping the covenant' on the part of Israel meant obeying the laws which God had given them.

THIRD, *the law defines the area within which God's people will experience the blessings of the covenant.* Obeying the law means keeping the covenant. Let's come back to our marriage illustration: if husbands and wives remain faithful to each other, they will enjoy the blessings and happiness which marriage promises. If a husband is unfaithful to his wife, then he remains married, but his unfaithfulness leads him into a web of deception, unhappiness and hurt which may take a long time to recover from. So God gave laws to his people which made it clear that the blessings of the covenant were related to the way their lives were to be lived. The path of obedience was the path of covenant blessing; the path of disobedience was the path on which blessings would be forfeited.

> The amazing thing is that ... God remains faithful to his covenant promise.

The amazing thing is that, in spite of the unfaithfulness of his people, God remains faithful to his covenant promise. Even when they broke his laws, God reiterated his covenant pledge to Moses, saying: 'The LORD, the LORD, a God merciful and gracious, slow to anger, and abounding in steadfast love and faithfulness, keeping steadfast love for thousands, forgiving iniquity and transgression and sin, but who will by no means clear the guilty ..' (Exod. 34:6-7).

Laws may be broken, but the covenant can never be broken.

One other thing: it is clear that the laws God gave to Israel were not all of the same kind. For example, Exodus 20:3-17 lists the laws we have come to call the Ten Commandments. They were obviously distinctive. God wrote them down on stone tablets and gave them to Moses at Mount Sinai. These are the laws which make up the Book of the Covenant (Exod. 24:7). We often refer to these as the *moral law*.

Other laws were given to Israel to regulate social matters: laws to do with slaves, with restoring lost property, laws regarding manslaughter, laws regarding lending and borrowing money—and so on. These were laws in which the moral standards of the Ten Commandments were applied to various situations in the lives of the people, and which regulated Israel as a nation. These can be described as Israel's *civil law*.

Then there were laws which regulated the way God was to be worshipped: laws, for example, regarding the Tabernacle and regarding the priests (Exod. 25-30). These laws governed the elaborate ritual which was required for Israel's religious devotion. These are often referred to as the *ceremonial law*.

One of the major divisions among Christians today is over the nature of God's law. Do any, or all, of these commandments still apply to us? At one extreme there are those who argue for the application of *all* the Old Testament laws to our lives, morally, socially and religiously. At the other, there are those who point to New Testament verses such as 'the law was given through Moses; grace and truth came through Jesus Christ' (John 1:17) or 'you are not under law but under grace' (Rom. 6:14) and argue that we are not under obligation to keep any of the Old Testament laws—unless the New Testament endorses them.

There are good reasons for believing, however, that the Ten Commandments, which are clearly stated as being identified with God's covenant, are still binding on us. When Jesus, for example, talks about 'the commandments', it is clear that it is the Ten Commandments he has in view (Luke 18:20). Similarly, when Paul talks about the law in Romans 7:7, he is referring to the Ten Commandments. In the age of the Holy Spirit, we are under God's covenant in a new way, in which God's law is written on our hearts (Jer. 31:33), meaning that we have a new desire and impulse to honour the laws of God in our daily lives. If we are Christians, we will be able to say, 'I love your law' (Ps. 119:113), or, as Paul puts it, 'I delight in the law of God in my inner being' (Rom. 7:22).

So, although we can profit from studying any and every part of the Old Testament—after all, 'all Scripture is breathed out by God and profitable for teaching, for reproof, for correction and for training in righteousness' (2 Tim. 3:16) —nonetheless we need to be careful in our handling of many Old Testament passages, making sure we interpret them in the light of other Scriptures. When we do so, I think we will see the truth of the following observation:

> Alongside the Ten Commandments, which enshrine eternal
> principles of conduct and have permanent validity, there was

a large corpus of additional law and it is this additional law that we say no longer binds the Christian. There was a great deal of liturgical law, bound up with the Temple and its ordinances. There was also a great deal of civil and political law. These laws were temporary and transitional. They depended on the Temple itself continuing to stand, on residence in the land of Palestine, on the wilderness journeys, and on the fact that one day Christ would come and fulfil the symbolism of Old Testament typology.[10]

So, bearing all this in mind, let's remind ourselves of these Ten Commandments which reveal God's moral authority, and must be the moral absolutes which regulate and modify all our behaviour. They can be summarized as follows:

Do not have any other god but me.

Do not worship me in any way other than the way I prescribe.

Do not use my name lightly.

Keep my day holy.

Honour your parents.

Do not kill.

Do not commit adultery.

Do not steal.

Do not tell lies.

Do not covet.

It is immediately clear that these ten words govern all of life. They regulate the religious life of man, and they regulate the personal and social life of man. They tell us how we ought to live in relation to God, and how we ought to live in relation to others. That order is important, because 'true morality is founded on reverence towards God'.[11]

FOR FURTHER STUDY

1. Compare 19:6 with 1 Peter 2:9. What can the Sinai experience teach us about the nature of Christ's church?

2. Read Hebrews 12:18-24. While there are comparisons and continuities between the Old and New Testaments, there are also contrasts and discontinuities. What use does the writer to the Hebrews make of the Sinai experience in this passage?

3. 'On the third day' God came down (19:11, 16). What does Matthew 16:21 highlight about 'the third day'?

TO THINK ABOUT AND DISCUSS

1. What makes the Ten Commandments special? How might they be applied in modern society?

2. How do the Ten Commandments help us understand the character of Jesus?

9 Obeying the King

(20:22-23:19)

God's people are to discover the practical implications of being in covenant with the King. If God is their King, he is to be obeyed. Obedience is the only way to blessing. Redeemed by him, they must now demonstrate their love to him by willing and glad obedience in every area of life and behaviour.

The Ten Commandments were not the only regulations God gave his people. They were certainly different, and distinctive laws, in addition to which, the moral principles they represent run through all the other pieces of legislation, which have to do either with Israel's religious worship or Israel's social living. That is why the next section of Exodus represents a variety of laws for a variety of situations.

The King gives laws

So what were the laws given by God to his people? They were:

Concerning altars (20:22-26)

An altar is a place of sacrifice and worship. God is to be worshipped only in the way that he demands and requires. He forbids idols of silver or gold to be crafted, because he is a spirit. His altar must be made either of earth or of uncarved stones, and there must be no elaborate stairway or step up to the altar. The emphasis is on simplicity, plainness and earthboundness.

Concerning slaves (21:1-11)

This law highlights the two themes that have already run through the book of Exodus: slavery and freedom, bondage and liberty. It also represents another application of the sabbath principle: after a slave had served his master for six years, he was to be offered his freedom in the seventh. It was possible that the slave loved his master so much that he did not wish to take advantage of this opportunity, in which case he

> **Obedience is the only way to blessing.**

could serve for life, with a hole bored in his ear as a sign of his pledge. Female slaves were in a different category, but the law did make provision for such slaves to be redeemed. Themes common to the book of Exodus run through this narrative.

Concerning behaviour (21:12-32)

Some sins, according to these laws, required the death penalty in ancient Israel. These included wilful murder, the murder or cursing of one's parents, and the abduction and enslavement of an individual. Other offences, such as quarrelling and hitting another man, or a slave, or a pregnant woman, were regulated for. So, too, were cases as diverse as knocking out the tooth of a slave, or what to do if your ox gores someone to death. The specific cases mentioned help to illustrate the absolute principles of the Ten Commandments, and highlight particular applications of these laws, which are to cover the whole of life. The basic principle, however, is that of verses 23-5: 'If there is harm, then you shall pay life for life, eye for eye, tooth for tooth, hand for hand, foot for foot, burn for burn, wound for wound, stripe for stripe.'

Concerning restitution (21:33-22:15)

In some cases, the offences were dealt with by restoration or restitution—paying the cost of the loss. If someone's beast fell into your pit or well, you had to meet the cost, or if your fire causes damage to a field of corn, you must pay. The Hebrew word 'elohim', usually translated 'God' in the Old Testament, could also mean 'judges', hence the different translations of Exodus 22:8-9; some talk of bringing the case before God (ESV), others before the judges (AV, NIV). The cases illustrate that God is a God of justice and order.

Concerning social life (22:16-23:9)

Various issues are dealt with in this category of laws. These include having sex with an unbetrothed virgin, bestiality, dealing with widows and orphans, lending money, consecration of the harvest, being party to a lie or false accusation, perverting the course of justice, and dealing with strangers. While a variety of situations is presented, some familiar themes emerge: 'You shall be consecrated to me,' God says in 22:31; 'You know the heart of a sojourner,' says God in 23:9, 'for you were sojourners in the land of Egypt.' Of particular interest is the phrase 'devoted to destruction' in 22:20, referring to a solemn, holy action in which someone or something is devoted to the Lord for his judgement. (Compare this with Joshua 6:18).

Concerning holy festivals (23:10-19)

Religious festivities and regulations are mentioned in this group of laws. These include the application of the sabbath principle, first to the harvest—the land is to lie fallow and 'sabbath' in rest every seventh year. The benefit of this is that the poor and homeless will have sustenance. Then the principle is applied to the weekly cycle of days, in which each seventh day is devoted to the Lord, as the fourth commandment requires. No other god is to be worshipped. Three annual festivals are also mentioned: the Feast of Unleavened Bread, the Feast of Harvest (also called the Feast of Weeks, or Pentecost), and the Feast of Ingathering (or Tabernacles). These are elaborated on in Leviticus 23. The requirement to bring the firstfruits of the ground to God is an extension of his claim over the first of everything (see 13:1). The prohibition against boiling a young goat in its mother's milk is obscure, but is a call to God's people to be different from all the nations round about.

For further study ▶

FOR FURTHER STUDY

1. The sign of a willing slave was a hole in his ear. How does this image help us to understand Psalm 40:6 and its subsequent citation in Hebrews 10:5-7?

2. The principle of 'an eye for an eye and a tooth for a tooth' is taken up by Jesus in the Sermon on the Mount in Matthew 5:38. How does his usage and teaching help us to understand the laws of his kingdom? How is Christian behaviour to be modified? Is Jesus teaching a different ethic?

3. Look at the following instances of places and people 'devoted to destruction'. Can you identify what or who are to be handed over to the Lord as offerings for judgement? Numbers 21:2, Joshua 2:10, Judges 1:17, 1 Samuel 15:3. The Greek word 'anathema', or 'cursed' seems to carry this idea into the New Testament. In this light, how do you interpret 1 Corinthians 16:22?

TO THINK ABOUT AND DISCUSS

1. Why does God give such detailed laws to his people? What does this tell us about the character of God, and the character of those whom he has redeemed?

2. The sabbath principle is prominent in these laws. Look again at the ways in which it is highlighted. How might we apply this principle in modern life?

3. Are these social and religious regulations relevant in any sense for the modern Christian church? Suggest some reasons or examples if you can think of any.

10 Covenant with the King

(23:20-24:18)

This King is full of grace! Here he ratifies his covenant relationship with his people, bringing them through formal rituals which serve to demonstrate publicly that they are his, and that he is theirs.

Following the body of laws given to the people, God now speaks about their conquest of the land of Canaan, and confirms his covenant with his people. This is an important section, in which the emphasis is on preparation for the future.

God's covenant pledge (23:20-33)

Although these verses describe events that will take place when the Israelites come into the land of Canaan, the form of speech is striking. On the one hand, most of the promised action is God's, not the people's. God will send an angel (v. 20), and he undertakes to fulfil their days (v. 26), send his 'terror' into the land (v. 27), drive out the inhabitants (v. 28), set the borders of the territory of his people (v. 31) and give them the land to inhabit.

On the other hand, these pledges appear to depend on their obedience. God will be an enemy to the enemies of his people if they obey him (v. 22). He will take sickness away if they serve him (v. 25). And their possession of the land is related clearly to their devotion to the Lord alone; they are not to make any covenant with the Canaanites or the gods of the Canaanites (v. 32).

> The King is looking for obedience from his people, not as the reason for which he will act on their behalf, but as the response on their part to what he will do for them.

This is very clearly the language of covenant, in which the covenant King undertakes to bring his people into the land, just as he said to Abraham (Gen. 12:1, 7). In doing so, the King, in his own strength and by his own grace, will fulfil his own promises to his people. To that extent, the covenant is entirely a covenant of grace.

Yet there are elements of conditionality within this covenant. Its fulfilment is not entirely dependent on the obedience and service of the people, but for them to enjoy the full benefits of what he is undertaking to do for them, they must obey him.

This passage, therefore, relates very closely to what has gone before. It is not to be read apart from the emphasis on law, for the King is looking for obedience from his people, not as the reason for which he will act on their behalf, but as the response on their part to what he will do for them.

There are one or two issues worth highlighting here. First, who is this 'angel' whom God promises to send before them, to guard them on their journey and whom they must obey? We know from the Bible that God made angels to worship him and to minister to his people (see Heb. 1:13-14). But this angel is different.

We need to understand this passage in the light of Genesis 16:7, where 'the angel of the LORD' appeared to Hagar, or Genesis 22:11, 15, where the same figure appears to Abraham. This angel is both distinguished from God, yet speaks as God. More importantly, Moses' great encounter at the burning bush was with the angel of the Lord (Exod. 3:2); there, the Lord's name was revealed, and here God says of the angel that 'my name is in him' (v. 21). As the scholar Geerhardus Vos puts it, 'the sending of "the Angel of Jehovah" could not have been represented as anything less than Jehovah's own going'[12]; in other words, the presence of this Angel *is* the presence of God.

The remarkable thing is that this Angel would speak to them and lead them to the land. In a wonderful, supernatural provision, God himself would be among his people, setting his commands before them, leading and guiding them, and enabling them to possess the land.

Second, the possession of the land of Canaan will mean that the Amorites, Hittites, Perizzites, Canaanites and Hivites will be driven out of the land. This raises an important moral question about the ethics of all this: how can it be right for God to dispossess the dwellers of Canaan in order to settle the Israelites there? Further, how can it be right for God to 'blot them out' (v. 23), and thoroughly disadvantage them?

94

One answer to the question is that God is not showing any capriciousness or malice against the individuals who live in Canaan; he is dealing with them as an entity, an entire race. That, however, does not really solve the moral dilemma.

Another response is to realize that the Canaanites were dispossessed as punishment for their own wickedness and idolatry. In Genesis 15:16, God had said to Abram that his descendants would inhabit the land when the iniquity of the Amorites would be complete. Now God is moving nearer to fulfilling that promise. The Canaanites will lose their land through sin; the Israelites will possess it through grace.

> There is...the Lord's intention to have a holy nation (*cf* 19:6) in the world, as a testimony to his existence and faithfulness, and out of which a Saviour for the whole world would come.

Coupled with this is the Lord's intention to have a holy nation (*cf* 19:6) in the world, as a testimony to his existence and faithfulness, and out of which a Saviour for the whole world would come. The Canaanites were a threat to that purpose of grace: 'Far greater mischief would have resulted if they had been permitted to live on in the midst of the Hebrew nation. These incorrigible degenerates of the Canaanite civilization were a sinister threat to the spiritual survival of Abraham's race'.13 That story will unfold as God fulfils his promise and the Old Testament history runs its course.

God's covenant people (24:1-8)

This, then, is the covenant word, a word of promise, of blessing and of hope. It now requires affirmation, acceptance and response. God's covenant people are required to pledge themselves to the acceptance of the terms of the King. That is the ceremony enacted here.

Three representatives of the tribes of Israel—Aaron, and his sons, Nadab and Abihu—accompany Moses into God's presence. They convey God's message to his people, and the people accept the terms of the covenant. Moses writes the words of God (v. 4), an important strand in the compilation of the five books of Moses, the first five books of the Bible. The importance of this is seen in the designation 'Book of the Covenant' in verse 7. This is how the people are to read God's law: it is the book of God's covenant, their guide for embracing all the promised blessings of God's covenant salvation.

The following morning, the people are consecrated in a ratification ceremony which begins with the building of an altar and the offering of sacrifices (v. 5). With the blood of the sacrifices, Moses sprinkles both the altar and the people, binding both together through the instrumentality of the blood. This solemn ceremony formally seals the relationship between God and his people. The reading of the book of the covenant and the sprinkling of the blood of the covenant define for them the nature of the bond of the covenant.

God's glory revealed (24:9-18)

The glory of the covenant King is further displayed on the

mountain, to which Moses and Aaron, Nadab and Abihu and seventy elders of Israel go up. There 'they saw the God of Israel'. What a gracious, glorious revelation of God this was. Ordinarily, no one could approach God and live; but now, God permits these representatives to come into his presence, and he lays no hand upon them for harm (v. 11), indeed, they eat and drink with him.

Moses, however, is permitted an even more glorious opportunity to engage in fellowship with God, and leaves the rest to enter into God's nearer presence. As the glory cloud rests on Sinai, God speaks to Moses out of the cloud, and he enters into God's presence, to be there for forty days and nights. This prepares us for the later comment with which the Book of Deuteronomy ends, that 'there has not arisen a prophet since in Israel like Moses, whom the LORD knew face to face' (Deut. 34:10).

FOR FURTHER STUDY

1. The promise of Matthew 28:18-20 is similar to the promise of God's presence in Exodus 23. How do they compare in their references to the name of God and to the responsibilities of God's people?

2. Read the account of the transfiguration of Jesus in Matthew 17:1-8. How does it compare to the events of Exodus 24? Who represented the people in the transfiguration account? Where does Moses feature? What part does a cloud play? Do the passages shed light on each other?

3. Read Hebrews 9:19-28, with its explanation of how 'the first covenant' was inaugurated with blood. How does it use the events described in Exodus 24 to illustrate the work of Jesus Christ for us?

4. What did Jesus mean when he used the words 'the blood of the covenant' in the inauguration of the Lord's Supper in Matthew 26:28?

TO THINK ABOUT AND DISCUSS

1. Are you aware of God's presence with you in the world? What are your responsibilities as a believer if you are to know God's blessing and presence in your life?

2. In what way can we be sprinkled with blood? (See Heb. 10:19-25 and 1 Peter 1:2.) What are Christians doing when they celebrate the Lord's Supper? Do you think there is a connection between the Lord's Supper and the eating and drinking referred to in v.11?

PART 4

Keeping the King's Company

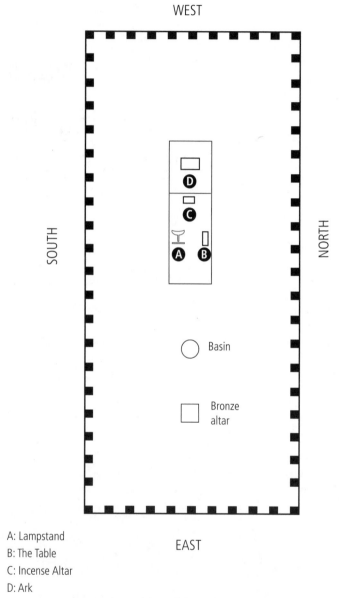

A: Lampstand
B: The Table
C: Incense Altar
D: Ark

WEST

SOUTH

NORTH

Basin

Bronze
altar

EAST

Groundplan of the Tabernacle

11 Holy places required: The Tabernacle

(25:1-27:21)

God's presence with his people is now to be established through a remarkable building programme. A special tent is to be constructed, in which the glory of God will be accommodated, and which will serve as the focal point of Israel's worship for the best part of a generation.

The next major section of Exodus is taken up with the Tabernacle, the special tent which God's people were asked to construct. In it, the glory which caused Sinai to shake, and to which the people could not approach, dwelt among God's people. The Tabernacle was the single most important element of their worship between Egypt and Canaan. It is also one of the dominant themes of the Pentateuch, since it is mentioned in eighteen chapters of Leviticus, thirteen of Numbers, and two of Deuteronomy.

The Tabernacle: an introduction (25:1-9)

There are three Hebrew words for the Tabernacle in the Old Testament. The first is *mishkan*, which means 'a dwelling-place'. It is used in 25:9, and is stated in 25:8 as the explicit purpose for which the tabernacle was to be erected: 'that I may dwell in their midst'.

A second word for the Tabernacle is the word *miqdosh*, which is used in 25:8 and means a 'holy (place)' *(cf* the use of sanctuary in 25:8 and tabernacle in 25:9). The Tabernacle was holy, as its two parts testify; one of these was termed a 'Holy Place' and the other the 'Most Holy Place'. Aaron, according to 28:36, was to wear an item on which was engraved the words 'Holy to the LORD'.

As we have seen, the theme of holiness is prominent in Exodus. According to the song of Moses in 15:11, God is 'majestic in holiness'. The nation of Israel was to be a 'holy nation' (19:6). Where God is, is holy. The essential teaching here is brought out in 29:43, where we read, '[the tabernacle] shall be sanctified by my glory'. The presence of the holy God, which caused the mountain to quake, sanctified the tabernacle and the people.

Thirdly, the Tabernacle is referred to as a '*tent*'—the ohel mo'ed, or 'tent of meeting'. In Exodus 40:2, Moses was commanded to construct 'the tabernacle of the tent of meeting'. This phrase is also used in 29:42, '...at the door of the tent of meeting before the LORD'. The word tent is also used to describe the Tabernacle in Numbers 9:15, where we are told that 'on the day that the tabernacle was set up, the cloud covered the tabernacle, the tent of the testimony [or witness]…' The tent was not only the place where the congregation of Israel assembled, but was also a witness to the Lord, since the Ark of the Covenant was there.

The concept of the tabernacle as a 'tent' is important, and reminds us of two things. First, the Tabernacle was a moveable and temporary structure. It was not fixed in any one location, and was constructed so that it could be carried about easily. This meant not only that the presence of God was among his people wherever they were; it was also a reminder that something permanent was necessary.

But, secondly, there was in the Tabernacle an identification of God with his people. They, too, dwelt in tents, as Hebrews 11:9 puts it, writing of Abraham, who, by faith, 'sojourned in the land of promise, as in a strange country, dwelling in tabernacles with Isaac, and Jacob, the heirs with him of the same promise, for he looked for a city which hath foundations, whose builder and maker is God' (AV). The presence of God in the Tabernacle was thus not only a symbol of God being among his people, but among them in a way that reflected his complete sympathy with them, and his identification with them.

There are three other preliminary factors to consider. Firstly, the construction of the Tabernacle was an *offering* to the Lord (v. 2). From the resources they had taken from the Egyptians in 12:30-36, the people are to construct this tent. Secondly, the offering was *willing* and *from the heart* (v. 2). Thirdly, the construction had to be according to God's design (v. 9). There was a regulative principle here: only what God commanded could please him.

We are going to pay attention to the individual elements of the Tabernacle. They are described twice in Exodus, in chapters 25-27, which moves from the centre of the tabernacle to the outside, and again in chapters 35-40, which describes the actual construction and moves from the outside in to the centre.

The Ark (25:10-22)

The first item for the Tabernacle was the Ark. It was the only item of furniture which would occupy three different places: the Tabernacle of Moses, the tent which David provided for it (1 Chron. 16:1) and Solomon's Temple (1 Kings 8:6).

The Ark was 3fi feet long, by 2/feet wide and high (111 x 67 x 67cm). It was constructed of acacia wood which is durable and non-perishable. This wood was to be overlaid with pure gold (v. 11) as distinguished from 'gold' (v. 12ff). The purity of the gold was a measure of its being refined, and was specifically used in materials central to the Tabernacle. This overlay was to be both inside and out, so that the appearance of the Ark was of solid gold. The Ark also had a crown of gold (as did the table of showbread (v. 24) and the altar of incense (30:3)). These trappings of sovereignty remind us that the purpose of the Ark was not merely to be a chest, but a throne—the King was dwelling among his people.

This is further revealed in the manner in which the Ark was to be transported. Two staves, again of acacia wood overlaid with gold, would be used to transport the Ark by means of four rings of gold in the four 'corners' (AV) of the Ark. It is possible that the word 'corner' could mean 'feet', which would mean that the staves on the shoulders of the priest would allow the Ark to tower over those who carried it, as a fitting emblem of the enthroned God. More importantly, the staves were to remain in the Ark until it was deposited finally in the Temple (see 1 Kings 8:8)

What did the Ark contain? According to verse 16, it contained 'the testimony that I shall give you'. That would imply the written tablets of the law (see 1 Kings 8:9). Hebrews 9:4 suggests that the Ark of the Covenant also contained the golden pot of manna and Aaron's rod that budded. A pot of manna was commanded to be laid up 'before the testimony to be kept' (Exod. 16:34). The same phrase is used in Numbers 17:10, when the Lord asked Moses to keep Aaron's rod 'before the testimony'. The writer to the Hebrews understood this to mean that these items were placed inside the Ark, and we have no reason to doubt this.

The important point was that the Ark was an Ark of Testimony, in which the law given in the theophany of Sinai, was housed.

The Ark was not open, however: a lid of pure gold was to be made for it. The Hebrew word is 'covering'; the phrase 'mercy seat' of verse 17 is the rendering of Martin Luther's German translation, which was adopted by William Tyndale. It is a paraphrase, drawn from the ritual which was carried out at this location.

The piece of gold which formed the covering for the Ark was to be shaped at either end into the form of an angel, or cherub, with the two cherubim stretching their wings over the covering and looking at each other. In Psalm 80:1, God is said to be enthroned between the cherubim. In 26:31, this is further emphasized with the image of cherubim upon the veil which separated the Holy from the Most Holy Place.

Verse 22 makes it clear that the Ark was the meeting-place, the place of fellowship and communion, and the symbol of the presence of the covenant God in the midst of his people. It was the symbol which gave meaning to the whole Tabernacle structure. It taught that the only way in which God and man may commune is on the basis of obedience to God's law and commandments.

The Table (25:23-30)

The Ark of the Covenant, containing the law and bearing the mercy seat, or atonement covering, was the only piece of furniture within the Most Holy Place. This was separated by a veil from the Holy Place, which contained three items.

The Holy Place was the place where the priests ministered daily. They represented the people, and were set apart for that purpose. They prepared the Table and ate its bread. They tended the lamp, which cast its glow upon the Holy Place. They looked after the altar of incense. And as they did so, they stood between the Most Holy Place and the Courtyard, between the place where the glory cloud of the Presence was, and the place where the court of the People was.

There is a similarity between the Ark of the Covenant and the Table for Bread. Both were made of acacia wood overlaid with gold. Both were of the same height (the only articles in the Tabernacle of which that was so). Both were surrounded and ornamented with a gold crown. Both had rings and staves for carrying. Both had something placed on them: the Ark had the mercy seat and the Table had the bread of the Presence. The Ark tells us of the ground of fellowship between God and man: atonement on the basis of righteousness. The Table speaks of the substance of that fellowship, and the effect of Christ's atonement: communion and fellowship with God through our feeding upon life-giving bread.

The Table was the place where bread was placed in the presence of God. Leviticus 24 speaks of this. The 'bread of the Presence' or 'bread of revelation' consisted of twelve loaves made of fine flour, baked and then placed in two rows on the Table. Pure frankincense was then sprinkled on the bread, which remained in the presence of the Lord for seven days. Each Sabbath day the bread was renewed and eaten by Aaron and his sons, by the priestly family, in the Holy Place.

Interestingly, just as the Sabbath pattern was established by the manner in which God created the world, so it was confirmed by the Lord in the wilderness. The manna was gathered each day, but not on the Sabbath. No bread came from God on the Sabbath, but bread had to be placed on the table before God in the Tabernacle every Sabbath. On the Sabbath day, the priestly family of Aaron ate the bread of that week. This was a remarkable provision for those who ministered before God.

The Lampstand (25:31-40)

The Holy Place was illuminated by a golden lampstand which bore seven lamps. The lampstand thus had two functions: to contribute to the splendour of the Holy Place (since it was made of gold) and to give light so that the priests could minister there.

The lampstand was to be constructed of pure gold, not an

overlay as with the Ark and the Table, but a beaten work of pure gold. Along with the lampstand, there were to be wick-trimmers, trays and lamps. These were all made from the one piece of gold, weighing a talent (75 pounds or 34 kilograms).

The lampstand, however, was to be a highly decorated and ornate item. It had one central stem rising from a base, out of which there were three pairs of branches, or arms. These are represented pictorially in different ways. Exodus 25:35 talks about buds, or calyxes, being on the stem under the point where the branches meet; the three pairs of branches are described similarly. Some take this to mean that the six branches were all the same length. If the branches were all the same length, then the lamps were at different heights. It is preferable however (and there seems to be later archaeological evidence for this) to imagine that the three pairs of branches were of different lengths, reaching up to the same height as the central stem, and resulting in all seven lamps being at the same height and casting light on the table.

The stem and the branches were rich in ornamentation. Each branch was decorated with three cups resembling almond blossoms (*cf* Jeremiah 1:11-12), each with calyx (the leaves covering the flower in bud) and flower. Four of these were also to decorate the central stem along with three calyxes under each pair of branches.

Life and growth are represented here, and there seems to be another connection made here between Tabernacle and creation. The candlestick, or menorah, points back to Eden's glory and represents the new creation through Christ's redemption. Just as there was a tree in the centre of the ancient Paradise, there is a tree in the Holy Place, and there will be a tree of life in the Paradise of God.

The function of this golden tree was to carry the lamps. The material for the lamps is not specified (v. 37). Perhaps they were clay lamps; at any rate they were to be filled with oil morning and evening, and their wicks trimmed each day to ensure light in the Holy Place continually. But the type of oil was specifically prescribed: it was to be pure olive oil, beaten for this purpose (Lev. 24:2) so that the lamps would never go out (Exod. 27:20).

The Curtains and Coverings (26:1-37)

The detail of the Tabernacle extended not only to the specific items of furniture which were integral to the priestly service, but also to the framework and coverings of the Tabernacle.

This is perhaps seen in the layout of the Tabernacle, where the rectangular structure was made of two squares of 50 x 50 cubits. It would appear that at the centre of one square was the altar of brass, and at the centre of the other the Ark of the Covenant.

There were two 'perimeter' walls to the Tabernacle. All the way around the outer court of the Tabernacle was a wall of linen, and around the sanctuary was a wall of gold, described in chapter 26.

This wall consisted of a framework of forty-eight boards of acacia wood overlaid with gold, reflecting the design of the Ark of the Covenant. Each of these boards stood in sockets of silver and they were held together with five bars on each of the closed sides of the sanctuary. The entrance to the Sanctuary had five pillars of gold with a linen curtain, and between the Holy Place and the Most Holy Place was a four pillar division, and another curtain of linen.

Curtains were hung in three places in the Tabernacle, to signify doors, or points of entrance. One was at the outside, and is called the gate of the Court (Exod. 38:18), one at the 'entrance to the tent' (v. 36), giving access to the Holy Place, and one within the sanctuary, dividing the Holy place from the Most Holy Place, called the veil (v. 31). All of these were made of blue, purple and scarlet.

There were also four coverings over the sanctuary.

The first was of linen (26:1-6). This was placed directly over the Holy Place and the Mosst Holy Place, and was the ceiling of the sanctuary. The linen curtain was also to be interworked with blue, purple and scarlet, as well as with the image of cherubim throughout.

This linen covering was made of ten curtains, each measuring twenty-eight cubits by four cubits. Five curtains were joined together into one large sheet; the two sheets were then tied with rings, and draped over the tabernacle. According to verse 6, the ten curtains became one tabernacle.

Above the linen covering was one of goats' hair (v. 7). This covering was made of eleven curtains—a number that seems to suggest sin, disorder and lawlessness. The goat was the animal for the sin offering on the Day of Atonement (Num. 28:22—'one male goat for a sin offering, to make atonement for you'). Five curtains covered the Most Holy Place, and this was joined with rings to the six curtains covering the Holy Place. Interestingly, the sixth curtain was to be folded back in the forefront of the tabernacle (v. 9). This eleventh curtain was the one which could be seen.

The third covering was that of rams' skins dyed red, or

tanned (v. 14). Rams were offered for the sin offering, the burnt offerings and the peace offerings. Its significance to the patriarchs was that of substitution—it was a ram which was slain on behalf of Isaac. This covering was placed over the goats' hair, and symbolized the fact that substitutionary blood was the only means by which contracted and actual guilt could be dealt with.

The final covering was of badgers' skins (v. 14, AV), for a final protection from heat and storm. No recorded measurements are given. And from the outside, no attraction, no fine embroidery, no colour, no cherubim are visible either. There is no comeliness, no beauty.

Perhaps the best way to have an understanding of the whole structure is to hear the conclusion of a sermon by C.H. Spurgeon on the silver sockets:

> Aye, but though the ingots were heavy to carry, every Israelite felt proud to think that that tabernacle had a foundation of silver. You Amalekites out there cannot see the silver footing of it all; you Moabites cannot perceive it. All you can see is the badger skins outside—the rough exterior of the tent. You say, 'That tent is a poor place to be a temple; that gospel is a very simple affair.' No doubt it is to you, but you never saw the silver sockets, you never saw the golden boards, you never saw the glory of the inside of the place lit up by the seven-branched candlesticks, and glorious with the presence of God. Brethren, redemption is our honour and delight. [14]

The Altar of Brass (27:1-8)

In the courtyard, as Professor John L. Mackay points out, 'less costly materials were used, the predominant metal being bronze, and the structure is less complex.' [15] This structure is also known as the altar of burnt offering, and is where sacrifices were made. It was a square shape, measuring five cubits by five cubits, and was three cubits high. It had the same proportion to the outer court of the Tabernacle as the altar of incense had to the Holy Place. One striking feature of this altar was that it had a horn on each corner, to which the sacrificial altar was tied (but see what other use could be made of it in 1 Kings 1:50-53). The basic structure was made of wood, overlaid with bronze, or brass. Regulation was made for all the utensils required for sacrifice—pans, shovels, basins, forks and pans. The fire for the altar was lit in a grate of brass under the altar. Like other furnishings, this altar had rings by which it could be carried on staves.

> A white linen wall marked the outer edge of the Tabernacle, and placed a line of demarcation and separation all around it. Amid the dust of the wilderness, the erection of this white linen wall must have been striking.

The description of the altar of incense is given in 30:1-10—please refer to the comments there to see the connection in worship between the two altars.

The Court (27:9-19)

The Tabernacle was one hundred cubits in length, and fifty cubits in width. On both sides along the length of the Tabernacle there were twenty pillars in sockets of brass, and along the breadth there were ten pillars on each side, making sixty pillars in all. It is perhaps not insignificant that sixty cubits was the length of the Temple (2 Chron. 3:3). These sixty pillars were joined together ('filleted') with connecting rods of silver, and the curtained linen wall was five cubits high.

A white linen wall marked the outer edge of the Tabernacle, and placed a line of demarcation and separation all around it. Amid the dust of the wilderness, the erection of this white linen wall must have been striking.

Oil for the Lamp (27:20-21)

A final regulation in this section concerns the need for lamps which needed to be tended daily. The fuel for these lamps was 'pure beaten olive oil', which the priests were required to maintain. The purity of the oil ensured that little smoke would be given off from the lamps.

For further study ▶

FOR FURTHER STUDY

1. Look up the following passages and consider what they tell us about the significance of the tabernacle: Psalm 61:4, Ezekiel 37:26-27, Revelation 21:3.

2. Read Hebrews 9:1-12. How does the writer to the Hebrews handle the material from Exodus? What use does he make of the tabernacle and its rituals? In what sense has Christ, our high priest, appeared 'through the greater and more perfect tent' (Heb. 9:11)?

3. In 1 Chronicles 28:2, the ark of the covenant is described as 'the footstool of our God'. What do you think this language conveys to us about God?

4. The regulations for the tabernacle reflect the complexity of Old Testament religion. What does John 4:24 tell us about the difference between that and New Testament religion? What is the modern equivalent of the tabernacle?

TO THINK ABOUT AND DISCUSS

1. In what sense was the death of Christ on the cross a sacrifice? (You might want to look up passages like Ephesians 5:2 and Hebrews 9:26.) In what sense are we as Christians to offer sacrifices? (Look at Romans 12:1, Philippians 2:17, Hebrews 13:15.)

2. In what ways is Jesus like the tabernacle?

3. How do the elements of the tabernacle help us better to understand the gospel?

12 Holy people required: the Priests

(28:1-30:38)

The worship of God is regulated to its finest details. The priests were the officials who were to minister in God's presence, and in God's tent. Their robes and the requirements for their consecration are clearly laid out by God. Every detail is important in this aspect of God's service.

In the same way that the Tabernacle was constructed by God according to a specific pattern and design, so the priests who were to minister there had to wear specific clothing, and be set apart to their office in a particular way.

Clothing the priests (28:1-43)

There were six main items to the priests' clothes: 'a breastpiece, an ephod, a robe, a coat of chequerwork, a turban and a sash' (v. 4). These garments were made of linen, and were embroidered and adorned with blue, scarlet and purple. Immediately we realize that there was a connection between the materials and design of the Tabernacle and that of the priests' clothing. Interestingly, too, no footwear is stipulated, relating to the command to Moses to remove his shoes on holy ground (3:5).

The chapter describes the ephod first (6-14), a simple garment hanging from the shoulders like a vest, with a representation of the twelve tribes of Israel on the shoulder pieces (vv. 9-10). The breastpiece (15-30) was also detailed, but its function was specific: it was 'a breastpiece of judgement' (v. 15), with stones representing the tribes of Israel, and the 'Urim and Thummim' (v. 30). Our knowledge of these is obscure, but by means of the Urim and Thummim decisions could be made in the presence of God. In the final blessing of Moses, these remain the property of Levi, and therefore of the priests (Deut. 33:8), and it is recorded in the time of Saul that God had not communicated with him by these means (1 Sam. 28:6).

The description of the robe follows (vv. 31-35). It was a single garment of blue, with decorative pomegranates and golden bells around the hem. The bells would signal Aaron's activity in the Holy Place.

An additional piece of information is given with the description of the turban, marked with the words 'Holy to the LORD' (v. 36), signifying the personal consecration of Aaron and the representative consecration of the people. The coat of chequerwork and the sash are made of linen, with linen undergarments to finish with.

Although some of these garments were worn by all the priests, the concentration of the chapter is on what Aaron, as

High Priest, must wear. Just as the priests represent the people, the High Priest represents the priests in the presence of God, and his work is the most important work on the Day of Atonement, when, once a year, he enters the Most Holy Place with blood.

Consecrating the priests (29:1-46)

In addition to the regulations covering the clothing of the priests come the requirements for consecrating the priests to their office. Although this is a long and detailed section, the rites of consecration focus on three activities.

FIRST is the activity of sacrifice and offering. A sin offering (10-14) and a food offering (15-18; 22-25) are to be offered to the Lord. In addition, a 'wave offering' of meat is offered to the Lord, and becomes a contribution from the people for the priests. Thus the priests who will offer sacrifices must have sacrifices offered for themselves, and those who will benefit from these sacrifices contribute to the wellbeing of the priests.

SECOND is the activity of clothing. The garments are placed on Aaron and his sons.

THIRD is the activity of anointing. Verses 19-21 describe the twofold anointing, with blood and with oil. They are to be anointed in their garments (v. 29), with the blood applied to their extremities: their ears, thumbs and big toes (v. 20).

This complex ritual lasted for seven days (v. 35), and also included the consecration of the altar (v. 37). In all of it, God was teaching his people that his presence made the tabernacle holy (v. 43).

The Altar of Incense (30:1-10)

In addition to the altar of brass, or bronze, in the courtyard, there was an altar of gold in the Holy Place. The altar of brass was for the offering of the burnt offering; the altar of gold was for the burning of incense in God's presence. There was clearly a connection between the two altars, one representing the consuming of an animal sacrifice, and the other the offering of a sweet smell. The importance of the golden altar is therefore related to the brass altar.

The golden altar of Incense was much smaller than the altar of brass. It was two cubits high, and one cubit square (almost three feet high by a foot-and-a-half square). As we have noted, however, they are in the same proportion to the place where they are housed. The brass altar of burnt-offering is five cubits square within the courtyard which is fifty cubits wide. The gold altar of incense is one cubit square within the Holy Place which is ten cubits wide. The width of each altar, therefore, is proportionately a tenth of the width of the part of the construction in which it is placed. This proportion highlights the connection between them.

The altar of incense was made of acacia wood, and was overlaid with gold. It had a horn in each corner, just as the brass altar did.

This altar was for the burning of incense, morning and evening perpetually (vv. 7-8). No 'strange incense' (v. 9, AV) was to be burnt upon this altar. The fate of Nadab and Abihu (Lev. 10), of Korah and his followers (Num. 16) and of Uzziah (2 Chron. 26:16ff) demonstrates that the duties of the altar of incense had to be regulated according to God's express command: that is, only the priests could perform the function, and only incense offered according to God's prescription would be acceptable.

This is reinforced in verses 34-8, where the precise combination of spices for the incense is detailed. The incense was to be holy and consecrated to the Lord. There is clearly an emphasis here on the Lord's jealousy for his own worship. But in addition, an interesting detail emerges. The principal element in the altar was *gold*; one of the elements (possibly the main element) of the incense compound was *frankincense*; and the main element in the oil of consecration, which was sprinkled on everything, including the altar of incense (30:27) was *myrrh*. It is not without significance that the same three elements appear in the birth narrative of Jesus.

What was the significance of the golden altar? By it, the Holy Place and the Most Holy Place were made fragrant, and the garments of the priests were impregnated with the fragrance. Following the destruction of the ancient world and the protection of Noah, Noah built an altar and the Lord smelled 'the pleasing aroma' (Gen. 8:21). Now, as then, the fragrance symbolized the acceptance of the offerings. Indeed, the language of pleasant aroma is frequently used of the sacrifices in Exodus (29:18, 25, 41), Leviticus (1:9, 13, 17; 2:2, 9, 12; 3:5, 16; 4:31 etc.) and Numbers (15:3, 7, 10, 13, 14, 24 etc.). The sacrifices were pleasant to God. They spoke of justice and atoning grace. They represented the basis upon which reconciliation was possible and atonement could be made.

Atonement Money (30:11-16)

Another interesting detail about the gold boards is the fact that they were set on silver sockets. Where did that silver come from? The answer is supplied here, where Moses was instructed to number the children of Israel. Every man over twenty years of age was commanded to bring half a shekel to the Lord 'to make atonement for your lives' (v. 15). This 'atonement money' (30:16) was paid individually and was then taken and used for making the sockets of the sanctuary. When Moses numbered the people, there were 603,550 men (38:26). If each of these gave half a shekel, that totalled 301,775 shekels. There were 3,000 shekels to a talent, and 100 talents were required for the tabernacle (ninety-six sockets for the walls and an additional four sockets for the pillars which upheld the veil—see Exodus 38:27). Thus each socket represented the redemption value of 6,000 people, and each board the redemption value of 12,000 people (the number sealed of every tribe in Revelation 7:1-8). The silver sockets represented the redemption of all of God's people, and this was the foundation of the sanctuary.

> C.H. Spurgeon is correct to say that the foundation of the worship of Israel was redemption.

C.H. Spurgeon is correct, therefore, to say that 'The foundation of the worship of Israel was redemption. The dwelling-place of the Lord their God was founded on atonement. All the boards of incorruptible wood and precious gold stood upon the redemption price, and the curtains of fine linen, and the veil of matchless workmanship, and the whole structure rested on nothing else but the solid mass of silver which had been paid as the redemption money of the people'.[16]

The Basin of Brass (30:17-21)

Another item of brass in the courtyard was the bronze basin, which held water in which Aaron and his sons would wash before service. This was not just so that they would be clean, but 'so that they may not die' (v. 20), and again highlights the importance of holiness on the part of those who will minister in the name and presence of the Lord.

Anointing Oil (30:22-38)

The final detail of the regulations governing the tabernacle is the prescription for the anointing oil and the incense. The oil was to be sprinkled on the tabernacle and all its furnishings and elements. It was itself holy (v. 32) and therefore could not be used for any other purpose. It also symbolized the consecration of all the parts of the tabernacle for God's glory and for God's service. The incense to be offered on the golden altar of incense is also described with detail, and the people are forbidden to put it to any other use.

For further study ▶

FOR FURTHER STUDY

1. In addition to being called our Passover, Jesus is also described as our 'great high priest' (Heb. 4:14, 8:1-7). How do the Tabernacle regulations help us to understand this description?

2. The following passages refer to incense. What do they compare incense to? Psalm 141:2, Revelation 5:8, 8:3.

3. How does the tabernacle help us to understand Christ's offering as 'a fragrant offering and sacrifice to God' (Eph. 5:2)?

TO THINK ABOUT AND DISCUSS

1. The name 'Messiah' or 'Christ' means 'anointed'. With what was Christ anointed (see Acts 10:38)? What significance does this have for the followers of Jesus? What do you think John means by 'the anointing you have received from him' (1 John 2:27)?

2. Paul uses tabernacle language in 2 Corinthians 5:1-2. What use does he make of it there? How should this enable us to live our Christian lives today?

3. In what sense should today's church be 'a royal priesthood' (1 Peter 2:9)?

13 Holy worship required

(31:1-35:3)

The work is about to begin. But the whole programme of events is interrupted by the false worship of the people, who make a god of gold and serve it. God is pleased only with the worship that he himself approves of.

The tabernacle was built for a particular reason, so that God would dwell among his people. This presence was the foundation of all the activity of the tabernacle, and draws our attention to the fact that the converse purpose of the tabernacle was that the people would dwell in the presence of God and worship him there. This section, in addition to giving further details on the construction of the tabernacle, reveals the reason why God must make provision for his own worship.

Workers for the Tabernacle (31:1-11)

God ordained the pattern of the tabernacle, and also chose the workers. They were Bezalel from the tribe of Judah, and

Oholiab from the tribe of Dan. We know very little about them. Their names ('Bezalel' meaning 'in the protection of God' and 'Oholiab' meaning 'father is a tent') could contain allusions to the tabernacle. What is more important is both their natural ability and the supernatural help they receive for this task; of Bezalel it is said that he has been filled with the Spirit of God for the purpose, a very unusual phrase in the Old Testament.

These were the main overseers of the whole project, and under them were a variety of craftsmen, who assisted in constructing the furnishings for the tabernacle and the clothing for the priests. Two guiding principles for the work are offered; on the one hand, they are to work within the guidance God has given, not introducing anything new or omitting any part of the work; on the other, they are able to design the artwork for the furnishings (v. 4) with a measure of freedom. But the emphasis falls on the fact that this is God's work; the design is his, the workmen are his, the equipping is his, so that all the glory will be his.

The Sabbath (31:12-18; 35:1-3)

Twice in this section there are passages dealing with the law of the Sabbath. Although these laws seem redundant in the context of the tabernacle regulations, they are clearly related. They suggest, for example, that no construction work for the tabernacle took place on the Sabbath. The sabbath principle modified the work principle. They also mandate the death penalty for Sabbath-breaking (v. 15).

More fundamental, however, is the fact that the Sabbath is related to God's eternal covenant (v. 16), as a sign of the relationship between himself and his people. This is not telling us that the Sabbath was merely an institution for ethnic Israel, for we know that its significance was wider than that. It was made for all men (Mark 2:27), not just for Israel. But it has especial significance for those who are in a covenant relationship with the Lord.

Another vital piece of information supplied here is the fact that the commandments were written on stone by the finger of God (v. 18). This was clearly the Book of the Covenant, the law of the ten words, which was to remain in the Ark of the Covenant (hence its connection with the tabernacle construction).

The importance of the Sabbath law is further emphasized in 35:1-3 when the people are ready for beginning work on the tabernacle. This will follow a period of apostasy and rebellion, showing even more clearly the need for a place for atonement, reconciliation and salvation. We cannot escape, however, the demands of a covenant God, whose name is holy, whose house is holy, and whose day is holy.

> It was the prolonged absence of Moses from them that caused the people to slip into idolatry. Tired of the wait, they persuade Aaron to frame a god for them. As they gladly parted with their golden jewellery, Aaron shaped a golden calf and called a feast to the Lord.

Defiling the worship of God (32:1-35)

According to Exodus, it was the prolonged absence of Moses from them that caused the people to slip into idolatry. Tired of the wait, they persuade Aaron to frame a god for them. As they gladly parted with their golden jewellery, Aaron shaped a golden calf and called a feast to the Lord. The calf was proclaimed to be the divinity which redeemed the people out of Egypt (v. 4). Thus in a stroke, the first two commandments were summarily dismissed: the people worshipped a false god, and tried to baptize it in the name of Jehovah, thus worshipping him in an ungodly and unjustifiable manner.

Thus, injected into the narrative of regulations and descriptions of the true worship of God is this narrative of false worship and of apostasy from the true God. The features of this false worship were its lack of spirituality, seriousness and holiness—the very qualities demanded by the God of Sinai.

God, however, was not unaware of what was going on. He is presented as calling Moses to leave him alone, that he may go down to consume these revellers in his anger (v. 10). That fact alone is striking—but no less is the realization that by doing so, Moses is permitted the opportunity to intercede on behalf of the recalcitrant and wayward nation.

Moses uses that opportunity well, basing his pleading on the covenant promises given to the patriarchs (v. 13), and God is presented as relenting from the fierceness of his anger (v. 14).

So is God like us? Not at all, but he does reveal himself and convey the truth about himself to us in ways that are accommodated to our understanding. He does not relent (1 Sam. 15:29) or change his mind, any more than he writes with literal fingers (31:18); but he reveals his purpose in ways that enable us to understand, and that integrate with a changing and faithless people.

Moses presents the people with the claims of Jehovah, but not without first expressing his own anger against them with the breaking of the stone tablets on which the laws of God were written. This was a highly symbolic gesture, which signified their unfaithfulness: they had, in effect, broken covenant with God and already displayed the tendency to spiritual adultery which would characterize them many times in the future.

And how pathetic is the excuse of Aaron! 'It's the people's fault,' he says. 'I just threw their gold into the fire, and this calf came out!' (vv. 22-24). How trite the explanation! How pathetic the excuse! This is the man whom God is going to set in the holy office of High Priest, yet he is ready to point the accusing finger away from himself to the people.

Moses' response is to call on the Levites to consecrate themselves to the service of God; those on the Lord's side are to step forward, they are given a sword, and they put to death about three thousand in Israel. God cannot be trifled with. The wages of sin is always death. He is not mocked (Gal. 6:7).

The following day, Moses brings the accusation before the people, but also speaks on their behalf to the God against whom they have sinned. Moses himself fulfils priestly, as well as prophetic, functions, in his ministry of intercession. Using the most solemn language, he urges God to forgive their sin, or else bring his judgement upon Moses himself to let the people go free. The same kind of language appears in Romans 9:3, where Paul expresses the solemn thought that he would rather be lost than see his fellow Jews perish without Christ. Such sentiments arise out of deep heart-love: 'The intensity of the apostle's love for his own people is hereby disclosed,' writes John Murray.[17] So, too, is the intensity of Moses' love for his own people revealed in verse 32.

The intercession is portrayed as modifying the response of the Lord. Instead of cursing and judging all the people, God sends a plague. Thus the demands of justice are met, the righteousness of God is vindicated, and the grace of God is revealed in the fact that, though three thousand perish, many more are spared.

Moses the intercessor (33:1-23)

The ministry of intercession for the people continues to be a major theme in the narrative, running into chapter 33. There are three main sections to this chapter.

FIRST, there is God's command to his people to leave Sinai. God gives the command, but he couples it with the threat that he will not go with the people, for fear that he will consume them for their sin. Moses commands them to take off their 'ornaments'.

SECOND, there is an account of what normally took place at the tent of meeting (vv. 7-11). This was a different construction to the tabernacle, and Moses pitched it 'outside the camp' (v. 7), presumably because of the sins of the people. The important thing to note is that in Moses the people had one who would bear their interests before God; with Moses, God spoke face to face as with a friend (v. 11). The reference to Joshua (v. 11) is an important indicator of the major role Joshua will later play as the successor of Moses.

THIRD, there is the account of the intercession of Moses, his appeals to God on behalf of wayward Israel. Moses has a twofold request. The first is 'show me your ways' (v. 13), and argues, on the basis of previous promises, that God's promise to his people was that he would accompany them. In this way, others would know that the Lord was with Israel (v. 16). Moses wishes to see something of God's character as the God whose purposes are honoured and whose promises are fulfilled.

The second plea is 'show me your glory' (v. 18). This is the formative principle of all that Moses is doing—that the glory of God will be revealed. The action is highly symbolic—God hiding Moses in a cave, passing by the cave, and permitting him the merest glimpse of the divine. To be exposed to the full revelation of that glory would be fatal (v. 20). The effect of this was that Moses' face shone with the reflection of God's grandeur (34:30).

Renewing the covenant (34:1-28)

The graciousness of Israel's God is the dominant theme here, as the covenant is renewed, and the Ten Commandments once again written down. The stone tablets which had been shattered to pieces as a result of what Moses saw in the camp of Israel are made again. The renewal of the covenant begins with the Lord's declaration of his character and his covenant pledge (vv. 6-7), following which Moses worships and pleads for forgiveness (v. 9).

Once again, the promise to dispossess the land of its

inhabitants is given to Israel, along with the conditions attached to the keeping of the covenant. These reiterate several of the commandments already given: no other god is to be worshipped (v. 14), no idol is to be framed (v. 17), the Feasts of the Lord are to be observed (v. 18), the firstborn is to be devoted to the Lord (vv. 19-20), the Sabbath is to be kept (v. 21), and so on.

A shining face (34:29-35)

Moses could not see it, but as he descended after being on the mountain in God's presence for forty days and forty nights, his face shone. The people were afraid to come near him, so he covered his face with a veil (v. 33). The pattern of Moses' ministry was that he would speak to the Lord with uncovered face, and to the people with a veil.

> In Moses' experience, the presence of the Lord was not inconsequential or without impact. Moses discovered that to speak to the Lord face to face had repercussions!

In Moses' experience, the presence of the Lord was not inconsequential or without impact. Moses discovered that to speak to the Lord face to face had repercussions! Yet he shows his meekness and humility in veiling his shining face to allow the people to hear what God had to say through him.

FOR FURTHER STUDY

1. The men God uses are equipped for, and called to, the task he has for them. What are the qualifications God requires of those who work in his church today? (See 1 Tim. 3, Titus 1.)

2. Look up the following passages which refer to God 'repenting' or 'relenting': Genesis 6:6, Jeremiah 18:8, Jonah 3:10. In what contexts does God 'change his mind'? And how does this tie in with 1 Samuel 15:29?

3. What use does Paul make of the incident of Moses' shining face and the veil in 2 Corinthians 3:7-18?

TO THINK ABOUT AND DISCUSS

1. Do you think there is such a thing as a 'call to the ministry'? Are men still called and commissioned to build up the church in the way that Bezalel and Oholiab were set apart to build the tabernacle?

2. Writing about materialism in the church, author John White said that 'the church has gone a-whoring after a golden cow. Not a calf, if you please, but a cow.'[18] Do you agree?

3. What does the phrase 'the glory of God' mean to you? How should it affect you? Do you pray with Moses, 'Show me your glory!'? Should you?

14 Holy work required

(35:4-40:33)

God's workers are chosen, and his plans have been drawn up. Now they must serve him by constructing the tabernacle. The importance of the tabernacle is seen in the way in which much of the detail already given is repeated in this section of Exodus.

The importance of the tabernacle is seen in this final part of the Exodus narrative, in which we have a record of the construction of the sacred tent. With varying detail, the same subjects are covered here—the furnishings of the tabernacle, the garments of the priests, the main men involved in the project—as have already been considered. In a sense, this is one of the crescendo passages: as they set to work to construct the tabernacle, the people of God are fulfilling one of the main reasons for their redemption: to worship God in the wilderness (5:1, 7:16).

Contributing to the work (35:4-29)

Moses calls for contributions for the construction of the tabernacle. These are of two kinds: material and personal. The materials required are to be donated by 'whoever is of a generous heart' (v. 5), and includes all the dyed yarns and oil, the wood and the stones. The personal contribution is made by 'every skilful craftsman' (v. 10), whose personal involvement is necessary to ensure that all the detailed items required will be made.

The response was overwhelming. Men and women whose hearts were stirred to contribute to the Lord's work brought what they could, from linen to dyed wool, stones to spices. The contributions were so great that Moses had actually to stop the people from bringing any more (36:6-7)!

The building begins (35:30-36:38)

Moses also formally declared Bezalel and Oholiab to be the chosen workmen for the construction. Along with the craftsmen, they were the ones called to this particular work. Chapter 36 tells the story of how the tabernacle was constructed, beginning with the curtains (vv. 8-19) and the frames for the tabernacle (vv. 20-30), the bars (vv. 31-34) and the veil (vv. 35-38).

The construction progresses

The story of the construction corresponds with the instructions already given. Exodus tells of the manufacture of the furnishings in the following order:

THE ARK (37:1-9)—see on 25:10-22

THE TABLE (37:10-16)—see on 25:23-30

THE LAMPSTAND (37:17-24)—see on 25:31-40

THE ALTAR OF INCENSE (37:25-29)—see on 30:1-10

THE ALTAR OF BURNT OFFERING (38:1-7)—see on 27:1-8

THE BRONZE BASIN (38:8)—see on 30:17-21

THE COURT (38:9-20)—see on 27:9-19

The materials used (38:21-31)

Interestingly, we are informed here that a record was kept of all that was used in the construction of the tabernacle, and who the principal workmen were. In addition, we are told about the redemption money, paid as a census tax (see on 30:13-14).

Making the garments for the priests (39:1-43)

The record of the priests' garments corresponds to the material in chapter 28, and describes the making of the ephod (vv. 2-7), the breastpiece (vv. 8-21), the robe (vv. 22-26), linen coats (vv. 27-29) and the turban with its engraved statement 'Holy to the LORD' (vv. 30-31).

Running through the narrative is the repeated phrase 'as the LORD had commanded Moses' (see for example vv. 1, 5, 7, 21, 26, 29, 31). This is further emphasized in the summary statement of verse 32: 'Thus all the work of the tabernacle was finished, and the people of Israel did according to all that the LORD had commanded Moses so they did'. Moses saw the work, and blessed the people (vv. 42-43), language that echoes the creation account (see Gen. 1:31; 2:3).

Completing the work (40:1-33)

In the previous sections, Moses is seen as overseer of the tabernacle construction: here, he is the main worker, who now sets up the tabernacle carefully, locating each piece with the precision demanded by God himself. He also consecrates each piece of furnishing so that it is formally consecrated to God, and set apart for his worship.

> Here, Moses is the main worker, who now sets up the tabernacle carefully, locating each piece with the precision demanded by God himself.

So, on the first day of the first month, 'Moses erected the tabernacle' (v. 18), arranging each item carefully, until he had 'finished the work' (v. 33).

For further study ▶

1. What does 1 Corinthians 16:1-3 say about contributing to the work of the church? How might Exodus 35:5 and 36:5-7 be realized in today's church?

2. Linen was a major element both in the tabernacle furnishings (36:8) and in the priestly garments (39:27-28). What does Revelation 19:8 say about linen? Does the tabernacle regulation help us to understand this better?

3. How does Hebrews 3:1-6 compare and contrast Moses and Jesus?

TO THINK ABOUT AND DISCUSS

1. There is clearly a relationship between the role of Moses and the role of the craftsmen. *Moses* is said to have completed the work of the tabernacle, although others were responsible for the craftsmanship. In the work of the church, what is the relationship between Jesus' work and ours?

2. Why do you think the Book of Exodus pays so much attention to the tabernacle? What is the reason for the intricate and minute detail?

3. If we are biblical believers, should we build a tabernacle for ourselves? What is the equivalent of the tabernacle for us?

CONCLUSION

Journeying into the Unknown

15 Into the future

(40:34-38)

At a marriage service, following the months of preparation and planning, I often say to the newly married couple that although the wedding has finally come, the marriage is just beginning.

In a sense, that's where we are at now, at the end of the Book of Exodus. The covenant promises are finally realized, to the extent that God's people are no longer in slavery. God has made them free. But the journey is just beginning. The tabernacle has been constructed. The tabernacle of God is with men. He dwells with them. They are his people. He is their God. Suddenly, the most glorious aspect of the whole construction becomes a reality: 'the glory of the LORD filled the tabernacle' (40:34). The glory Moses saw at the beginning in chapter 3, the glory that descended on Sinai in chapter 19, the glory that passed by Moses in chapter 33—that glory now descends to dwell in the midst of God's people.

They moved forward as and when the glory-cloud led them on. When the glory-cloud rested, so did they. In all their journeys, they experienced the blessed, glorious presence of the living God. Who could not be excited about the journey, now that God made his abode among his own people?

I once spoke to a young man in my congregation who had emerged out of a particularly difficult experience. It was an experience he described as 'a black place', and it was not easy for him to recount it. But he began to pray and to seek for Jesus, and God delivered him. When I spoke to him, he said, 'I am excited about the future!' The past was gone; something better lay ahead.

That's where we leave God's people, redeemed by grace, heading out in faith, led by God, fortified by his presence, guided by his hand, 'seeking a homeland' (Heb. 11:14). Like them, we must move forward too, facing the trials of wilderness life, knowing that 'if God is for us, who can be against us?' (Rom. 8:31).

'Therefore, let us go to him outside the camp and bear the reproach he endured. For here we have no lasting city, but we seek the city that is to come' (Heb. 13:13-14).

Will you make this journey of faith—this journey of a lifetime?

Endnotes

1 Geerhardus Vos, *Biblical Theology*, Eerdmans: Grand Rapids, MI, 1971, p162

2 O.P. Robertson, *The Christ of the Covenants*, P&R: New Jersey, 1980, p198

3 For a good discussion of this, one of the best places to look is in John L. Mackay's *Commentary on Exodus*, published by Mentor in 2001 (especially pp13-20)

4 G.L. Archer, *Encyclopedia of Bible Difficulties*, Zondervan: Grand Rapids, MI, 1982, p198

5 Robertson, *Christ of the Covenants*, p6

6 John Owen, 'The Glory of Christ in the Constitution of his Person', Works, Vol 1, p311

7 See the discussion in W. C. Kaiser, *A History of Israel from the Bronze Age Through the Jewish Wars*, Broadman and Holman, Nashvilee, TN: 1998, pp96-101

8 John L. Mackay, *Exodus*: A Mentor Commentary: Fearn, 2001, p211

9 See the discussion in Kaiser, *A History*, p102 for the integrity of the statement of numbers

10 Donald Macleod, *A Faith to Live By*, Mentor: Fearn, 1998, p186

11 Mackay, *Exodus*, p342

12 Vos, *Biblical Theology*, p122

13 Archer, *Encyclopedia of Bible Difficulties*, p158

14 C.H. Spurgeon, *Jesus Christ: The History, Ceremony and Prophecy as told in the Old Testament*, AMG Publishers, 1994, p292

15 Mackay, *Exodus*, p466

16 Spurgeon, *Jesus Christ*, p284

17 John Murray, *The Epistle to the Romans*, Vol 2, NICNT, Eerdmans, Grand Rapids: 1965, pp3-4

18 John White, *The Golden Cow*, Marshall, Morgan and Scott: London, 1979, p55

OPENING UP EXODUS

The Opening up series

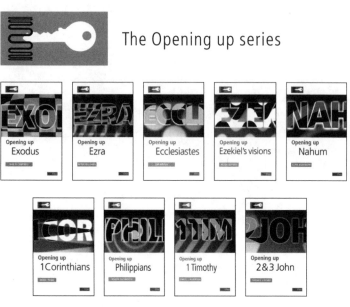

Opening up
Exodus

Opening up
Ezra

Opening up
Ecclesiastes

Opening up
Ezekiel's visions

Opening up
Nahum

Opening up
1 Corinthians

Opening up
Philippians

Opening up
1 Timothy

Opening up
2 & 3 John

Further titles in preparartion

This fine series is aimed at the 'average person in the church' and combines brevity, accuracy and readability with an attractive page layout. Thought-provoking questions make the books ideal for both personal or small group use.

'Laden with insightful quotes and penetrating practical application, Opening up Philippians is a Bible study tool which belongs on every Christian's bookshelf!'

DR. PHIL ROBERTS, PRESIDENT, MIDWESTERN BAPTIST THEOLOGICAL SEMINARY, KANSAS CITY, M I S S O U R I

Please contact us for a free catalogue

In the UK ☎ 01568 613 740   **email—** sales@dayone.co.uk

In the United States: ☎ Toll Free: 1-8-morebooks

In Canada: ☎ 519 763 0339 www.dayone.co.uk